AF512313

Partnering Together for a Secure Maritime Future

Partnering Together for a Secure Maritime Future

Editors

Vijay Sakhuja
Raghavendra Mishra

National Maritime Foundation

KNOWLEDGE WORLD
KW Publishers Pvt Ltd
New Delhi

Copyright © 2016, National Maritime Foundation.

All rights reserved. No part of this publication may be reproduced, stored in a retrieval system, or transmitted in any form or by any means, electronic, mechanical, photocopying, recording or otherwise, without the prior written permission of the copyright owner. The views expressed in this book are those of the contributors in their personal capacity and do not have any official or institutional endorsement.

ISBN 978-93-83649-94-5

Published in India by
Kalpana Shukla
KW Publishers Pvt Ltd
4676/21, First Floor, Ansari Road, Daryaganj, New Delhi 110002
T: +91.11.23263498 / 43528107 E: knowledgeworld@kwpub.com W: www.kwpub.com

Printed and bound in India by Nutech Print Services-India

Cover photograph courtesy Commander Navtej Singh, Indian Navy

Contents

Section II
Regional Perceptions and Approaches for Maritime Cooperative Engagements

Address by Shri Narendra Modi, Hon'ble Prime Minister of India, at the International Fleet Review

Honourable Governor of Andhra Pradesh and Chief Minister; my Cabinet colleagues; Delegates of Foreign Navies; Brave and proud men and women of the Indian Navy and the resolute people of this great city—Visakhapatnam. I am privileged to visit Visakhapatnam. This city has a special place in the heart of all Indians.

My last visit to Vishakhapatnam was in October of 2014. At that time, Cyclone Hudhud had left the city shattered in pieces. But, the people of Vishakhapatnam smiled in the face of adversity. It is a tribute to the city that within 14 months, you have risen against all odds to welcome navies from across the continents in this International Fleet Review.

A little over a year ago, we saw the full fury of the ocean. Today, thanks to the spirit of the people of Visakhapatnam, we are discussing how the oceans can be a source of economic prosperity for all of us. For its courage and resolve, we all salute the city of Visakhapatnam. My profuse thanks to the men and women of the Indian Navy for their tireless dedication towards making this Fleet Review a truly historic success. My sincere gratitude also to Chief Minister Chandrababu Naiduji for his strong support for this international event.

For me personally, witnessing the harmony among the best of international navies here has been a rewarding experience. Just over three months earlier in October, we welcomed in New Delhi, for the first time ever, all the 54 African Nations, including over 40 Heads of State for the 3rd India-Africa Summit. A few weeks earlier in August 2015, India had hosted in Jaipur 14 Heads of the State for the Second Forum for India-Pacific Island Cooperation. Just day before yesterday, we welcomed all the SAARC countries for the 12th South Asian Games in Guwahati. And today it is our pleasure to welcome 50 foreign navies from every corner of the globe at India's second International Fleet Review—the first one on India's east coast.

Your participation is a message of cooperation and friendship that we deeply cherish. On behalf of my countrymen, I thank you all for accepting our invitation and joining in this event with such spirit. To build on the gains from today's gathering, India would host the first-ever Global Maritime Summit in April this year. Its priority would be to scale up and strengthen the vibrant trade, investment, technology and commercial linkages between India and other maritime nations.

Friends, the oceans and world's waterways are global commons. *Vasudhaiva Kutumbakam*—the concept of the whole world as a family—is perhaps most vividly witnessed on the oceans of the planet that connect us all. The last time India hosted the International Fleet Review was in the year 2001, in the city of Mumbai. The world of 2016 is vastly different. Its politics is turbulent and its challenges, complex. At the same time, oceans remain the lifelines of global prosperity. They present us with great economic opportunities for building our nations.

Over 90% of the global merchandise trade is carried through the oceans. Over the last 15 years, its value has grown from about 6 trillion dollars to about 20 trillion dollars. Oceans are critical for the global energy security as over 60% of the world's oil production moves through sea routes. Our ability to reap economic benefits from the oceans rests on our capacity to respond to the challenges in the maritime domain.

The threat of seaborne terror, of which India has been a direct victim, continues to endanger the regional and global peace and stability. Piracy too remains a strong challenge. The threat of natural disasters like tsunamis and cyclones is ever present. Manmade problems such as oil spills, climate change, etc., continue to risk the stability of the maritime domain. A peaceful and stable maritime environment is, therefore, critical for regional and global security. It is also a must to harvest the riches of the oceanic ecosystem.

Given the scale and complexity of modern-day challenges, international maritime stability cannot be the preserve of a single nation. It has to be a shared goal and responsibility of all the seafaring countries. To this end, navies and maritime agencies of the world need to work together and engineer virtuous cycles of cooperation. But, where necessary, they also need to act to secure the international sea lanes of communication.

I believe that if oceans were to propel our economies, then we must:

- Use seas to build peace, friendship and trust, and curb conflict
- Respect and ensure freedom of navigation
- Cooperate, not compete, in responding to challenges on the sea

The large presence of foreign navies at this Fleet Review is a confirmation of our shared urge to walk the pathways of peace and cooperation in order to keep the maritime domain safe and secure.

Friends, India is, and has always been, a maritime nation. India's ancient Sanskrit texts also refer to the oceans as the storehouse of '*Chaturdashanam Ratnanam*', i.e., the 14 gems. Surrounded by sea from three sides, India has a long coastline of over 7500 kilometres. We have been blessed with a rich maritime heritage ever since Lothal in Gujarat became one of the earliest seaports of the world.

India's central location in the Indian Ocean has connected us with other cultures, shaped our maritime trade routes, influenced our strategic thought and defined our maritime character. Since the days of the Indus Valley civilisation, India has maintained an extensive network of maritime links, including with Africa, Western Asia, the Mediterranean region, the West, South East Asia and the Far East.

We are delighted that navies from all these regions have joined in this Fleet Review. The Photo Essay book on the 'Maritime Heritage of India' that I have just released, showcases this glorious maritime tradition.

Friends, in modern times too, the oceans, especially the Indian Ocean, occupy a vital place in India's national security and economic prosperity. The waters of the Indian Ocean touch the shores of over 40 countries. About one half of the world's container traffic and close to one-third of the world's cargo traffic passes through this region. 90% of our trade by volume and 90% of our oil imports are carried on the oceanic waters. India's 1200 island territories and our huge Exclusive Economic Zone of 2.4 million square kilometres makes clear the economic significance of the Indian Ocean.

For us, it also serves as a strategic bridge with the nations in our immediate and extended maritime neighbourhood. In March last year, in Mauritius, I had spelt out our vision for the Indian Ocean. The Indian Ocean Region is one of my foremost policy priorities. Our approach is evident in our vision of "Sagar", which means "Ocean" and stands for Security And Growth for All in the Region.

We would continue to actively pursue and promote our geopolitical, strategic and economic interests on the seas, in particular the Indian Ocean. To this end, India's modern and multidimensional navy leads from the front. It is a force for both peace and good. A network of growing political and economic maritime partnerships and strengthening of regional frameworks also helps us pursue our goals.

Friends, India's quest for economic prosperity through the oceans is a part of our larger efforts to transform India. We are not just a bright spot in the global economy. Regionally and internationally, we are a pillar of stability and an important growth centre. India's rise is in harmony with the goal of maintaining the regional and global peace and security.

Within the country, there is great optimism, enthusiasm and a "can do" mindset.

This optimism comes from the energy and enterprise of our confident youth. It also comes from our bold and sustained measures to transform our country, improve our laws, processes and institutions. We are launching new initiatives and creating opportunities to empower the people, giving them a sense of ownership in the nation's progress.

One of these is the "Make in India", where defence manufacturing and shipbuilding constitute some of its focus areas. In a week from now, on 13 February, we would hold seven days of global engagement under "Make in India" in Mumbai. During this time, the best in the global industry would link up with the innovation, design and manufacturing opportunities of India — the world's fastest growing economy. We want to invite the world to Make in India, Make for India and Make for the World. We take pride in the fact that of all the Indian naval ships participating in this Fleet Review, at least 37 are "Made in India" — a number that will surely rise in the coming years.

Our "Skill India" programme is building institutions that train, support, encourage and guide our 800 million youth on the path of entrepreneurship. Our skilled youth are ready to respond to the national and global manpower demands of the twenty-first century.

An important part of India's transformation is my vision of "Blue Economy". The blue *chakra* — or the wheel — in our National Flag, represents the potential of the Blue Economy. An essential part of this pursuit is the development of India's coastal and island territories: but, not just for tourism.

We want to build new pillars of economic activity in the coastal areas and in the linked hinterlands through a sustainable tapping of the oceanic resources. Strengthening our marine research and the development of an eco-friendly, marine industrial and technology base along with fisheries are other elements of our goal. In this endeavour, I see youth in the coastal areas as our true assets. They have a natural and deep understanding of the oceans. They could lead the way in the development of the Blue Economy in India. In partnership with all the coastal states of India, I want to shape a special programme for skilling India's youth in the coastal areas of the country.

Friends, in the end, let me once again congratulate the Indian Navy for the flawless conduct of this grand event. For the homeward journey of all our naval friends from across the world, may you always have fair winds, following seas and many a fathom below your keel.

Thank You.

Jai Hind!

[Editor's Note: The text of Prime Minister's address is available at http://pmindia.gov.in/en/news_updates/text-of-pms-address-at-international-fleet-review-2016/?comment=disable; rearranged and adapted for publication.]

Keynote Address by Shri Manohar Parrikar, Hon'ble Raksha Mantri at the International Maritime Conference

It is an honour and a privilege to deliver the Keynote Address to this august gathering at the International Maritime Conference, organised by the Indian Navy as part of the International Fleet Review 2016. I take this opportunity to extend a very warm welcome to all our guests from across the oceans, for being here at the 'City of Destiny', Visakhapatnam, and compliment the Indian Navy for its initiative to bring together the collective wisdom of the world navies under one roof.

Although land is the primary habitat of mankind and central to the political, economic, military and social activities, history bears out that the oceans have always, directly or indirectly, influenced events on land. In the present day and age too, the oceans are increasingly being looked upon as a resource provider and critical contributor to national growth and prosperity. The oceans are indeed the primary pathways of international trade and central to the global economy. These aspects are driving a steady, global shift of attention from land to the seas clearly exhibiting an expanding maritime outlook.

India's central position in the Indian Ocean Region (IOR), extended coastline, large Exclusive Economic Zone (EEZ), traditional economic pursuits and civilisational links make it a maritime nation whose prosperity and strategic independence are closely linked to the seas as it emerges on the international arena as a vibrant and self-assured nation in the twenty-first century. In safeguarding and promoting national security in the maritime domain, the Indian Navy is the principal instrument and manifestation of India's seapower.

Over the years, the Indian Navy has evolved systematically and impressively in size and capability, commensurate with its expanding mandate and growing significance to national security. The Navy's operating environment today is dynamic yet fragile, and demands a credible capability, enhanced readiness and constant presence at vital locations. This is true for the other navies as well. The current strategic environment continues to pose a wide spectrum of challenges and the blurring of lines between traditional and nontraditional threats requires a seamless and holistic approach towards maritime security to ensure that the seas remain secure and free for use by all.

The threats and challenges present today in the Indian Ocean are wide and diverse. A number of bilateral and multilateral initiatives are in place for carrying out synergised, inclusive and cooperative efforts. The Indian Ocean Naval Symposium (IONS) initiative launched by the Indian Navy in 2008, has now grown to 22 members who have signed the Charter of Business, with other four countries having joined as Observers.

Similarly, the Milan, a biennial series of interactions organised by the Indian Navy, has helped enhance regional cooperation and cooperative maritime engagement with navies from India's extended neighbourhood of Southeast Asia, Australia and New Zealand. These interactions are a milestone towards enhancing confidence among those navies and for building an enhanced safety and security framework at sea.

India's relations with the nations in our wider neighbourhood and beyond are an important facet of its politico-economic engagements and the Indian Navy plays an important role. Our focus has facilitated a conducive environment for development; at another level, India's endeavours, be it the 'Make in India' initiative or the 'Digital India', can provide opportunities for engaging a large community of stakeholders in order to strengthen peace and stability.

I am proud to say that the Indian Navy remains prepared to respond to emerging contingencies across the full spectrum of threats and challenges with alacrity and readiness, as displayed during the conduct of Operation Neer in Maldives in December 2014 and Operation Rahat in Yemen, last year.

The International Fleet Review 2016, with the theme of 'United through Oceans', offers us a unique opportunity towards 'Partnering Together for a Secure Maritime Future'. With this as the theme for the International Maritime Conference, I am sure that the event will provide an ideal platform for sharing experiences and perspectives and for brainstorming and broadening horizons for newer and efficient ways for securing a safe maritime future.

I wish complete success for all the healthy deliberations during the Conference. As you set sail for your homes in a few days, I also wish you fair winds and following seas. May the Gods of the Oceans be auspicious unto all those who sail upon them.

Jai Hind.

[Editor's Note: Adapted from the remarks made during the Keynote Address delivered on 07 February 2016 at the IFR Conference.]

एडमिरल आर के धवन
पी वी एस एम, ए वी एस एम, वाई एस एम, ए डी सी
नौसेनाध्यक्ष
Admiral RK Dhowan
PVSM, AVSM, YSM, ADC
Chief of the Naval Staff

रक्षा मंत्रालय
एकीकृत मुख्यालय (नौसेना)
नई दिल्ली-110011
Integrated Headquarters
Ministry of Defence (Navy)
New Delhi - 110011

MESSAGE

The seas around us are gaining ascendancy in the geopolitical, geo-economic and geostrategic matrix and the current century has been described as the century of the seas. While that maybe so, the threats and challenges in the maritime domain are wide and varied, and the seas are no longer a benign medium. It is also an established fact that no individual nation or navy is capable of ensuring the safety and security of the global commons. Given this milieu, the international character of oceans lends itself to cooperation where peace and stability is a shared responsibility, which is best achieved through collaborative approaches.

Global maritime partnerships and networking among navies are emerging as the new paradigm for the twenty-first century. Three important topics that resonate with the subject of 'Partnering Together for a Secure Maritime Future', the theme for this Conference, are: information exchange for a networked Maritime Domain Awareness (MDA); evolving collaborative institutional approaches to maritime security and a cooperative framework for enabling a collective response to Humanitarian Assistance and Disaster Relief (HADR). In this regard, the navies and other maritime enforcement agencies have the unique responsibility of keeping the seas safe and secure.

At the strategic level, the Indian Ocean region has emerged as the world's centre of gravity. Further, the littorals of this region are essentially oceanic in character with a natural outflow towards the sea with vast maritime interests. The inherent dynamics of this region also imply that any impediment to the free movement of seaborne commerce would impact not just the economies of the region, but the global economies as well. Consequently, safety, security and stability in the Indian Ocean is of paramount importance for the well-being and prosperity of all nations.

There is no doubt that fostering maritime partnerships is the way forward in promoting greater convergences towards evolving an equitable, inclusive and holistic maritime security architecture.

The compilation of papers and presentations in this book, through the collective wisdom of eminent participants of the International Maritime Conference at Visakhapatnam during the IFR 2016, organised under the aegis of the National Maritime Foundation, will go a long way in generating a meaningful discussion and in finding sustainable solutions to chart a collective course for the future.

Jai Hind.

(R. K. Dhowan)
Admiral
Chief of the Naval Staff

15 March 2016

Foreword

Late Sardar K. M. Panikkar, an eminent Indian historian-diplomat sometimes referred to as the Indian Mahan, wrote about 65 years ago: "The waters of the world form one vast expanse. While the land may be enveloped by the sea and the continents are so enveloped - the oceans are divided only by artificial boundaries". Those closely related with maritime issues would agree that this quote reflects the character of the oceans in that they remain truly the oldest global commons.

An overview of history would also show that seas have shaped and in turn, have been shaped by human endeavours. Human development and evolution, economics, international relations, exchange of ideas, spread of socio-cultural norms and knowledge, religion and beliefs across the globe have been facilitated by the medium of water. To be fair, oceans have also been a favourite playground of power politics, conflict and—in some cases—a means for subjugating others.

Changing tack from history to the present and looking into the mystery that is the future, there are three trends that are noteworthy. The first is the globalised nature of international affairs and strategic transactions. It is not as if a globalised world did not exist earlier, except for the fact that the world today is far more open, permissive and not divided into discrete blocs/alliance structures. Further, this globalisation extends across a new political geography of more than 190 nation states, which are equal stakeholders in shaping the future security architecture. In a similar vein, the oceanic regime of reducing jurisdiction as one moves away from the coast, with all seafaring nations being equal partners or players in its health, wealth and usage, is reflective of the enmeshed politico-economic construct of today.

Second, in this interconnected world, the oceans still carry 90 per cent of international commerce by volume and 70 per cent by value. The seas, therefore, remain the global economic arteries and sinews of the world. Further, the maritime industry is also considered as one with the largest globalised intent; one estimate putting this content at roughly 70 per cent.

The third and the last trend which needs reiteration is the rising global consciousness about the maritime domain be it in politico-diplomatic, economic or military-strategic terms, besides other nontraditional nonmilitary dimensions such as resource management and environmental effects.

Within this complex oceanic milieu, the grey and the white hulls, i.e. the navies and the coast guards for the International Fleet Review 2016 (IFR 16), play an important part in preserving the international character of the seas and ensuring a good order at sea. These maritime military forces not only safeguard the national interest of respective countries by providing credible tools for defence, deterrence and political signalling, but also contribute in equal measure—if not more—to regional as well as international security and stability. Some recent examples include the international response to the 2004 Tsunami, cooperative efforts to suppress piracy off the Horn of Africa, multinational search operations for the MH 370 and the evacuation of a stranded populace from some trouble spots in the Middle East where those evacuated included citizens of other countries as well.

At another level is the shift in the global strategic centre of gravity to the East, part of a maritime-configured region, which is seen from two lenses: one as the 'continuum of prosperity', whereas others describe it as 'an arc of instability or crisis'. It is with this background that the National Maritime Foundation, in concert with the Indian Navy, chose the theme of this event.

This volume emerges from the thoughts of domain experts who had been invited to the two-day international conference during IFR 16.

The volume has many takeaways for the readers at the policy, institutional and functional levels. I hope that this work would engender a better understanding of partnerships at sea for a stable and secure maritime future.

Admiral **D. K. Joshi**
PVSM, AVSM, YSM, NM, VSM (Retd)
Chairman,
National Maritime Foundation

Date: April 2016
Place: New Delhi

Abbreviations

AAA	American Arbitration Association
ADB	Asian Development Bank
ADMM	ASEAN Defence Ministers Meeting
AIIB	Asian Infrastructure Investment Bank
AMF	ASEAN Maritime Forum
ARF	ASEAN Regional Forum
ASEAN	Association of Southeast Asian Nations
bpd	barrels per day
BRI	Belt and Road Initiative
CBM	Confidence Building Measures
CGPCS	Contact Group on Piracy off the Coast of Somalia
CMF	Combined Maritime Forces
CoC	Code of Conduct
COLREGs	International Regulations for Preventing Collisions at Sea
COP21	21st Meeting of Conference of Parties on Climate Change
CPGS	Common Public Good Service
CUES	Code for Unalerted Encounters at Sea
DARPA	Defense Advanced Research Projects Agency
DoC	Declaration on the Conduct of Parties in the South China Sea
DPRI	Defence Policy Review Initiative
EAMF	Expanded ASEAN Maritime Forum
EAS	East Asia Summit
ECS	East China Sea
EEZ	Exclusive Economic Zone
EIA	Energy Information Agency
EiS	Eyes-in-the-Sky
EU	European Union
EWG	Experts Working Group
FON	Freedom of Navigation
GCC	Gulf Cooperation Council
HA/DR	Humanitarian Assistance/Disaster Relief
ICC	International Chamber of Commerce
ICDR	International Centre of Dispute Resolution
ICJ	International Court of Justice
ICSID	International Centre for the Settlement of Investment Disputes
IEG	Intelligence Exchange Group

IMB	International Maritime Bureau
IMO	International Maritime Organization
INCSEA	Incidents at Sea
IONS	Indian Ocean Naval Symposium
IOR	Indian Ocean Region
IORA	Indian Ocean Rim Association
ISR	Intelligence, Surveillance and Reconnaissance
ITLOS	International Tribunal for the Law of the Sea
JCC	Joint Coordinating Committee
JMSDF	Japanese Maritime Self-Defence Forces
LCIA	London Court of International Arbitration
Malsindo	Coordinated Patrols by Malaysia, Singapore and Indonesia
MIP	Maritime Infrastructure Protection
MSP	Malacca Strait Patrols
MSR	Maritime Silk Road
NATO	North Atlantic Treaty Organisation
NDPG	National Defence Program Guidelines
NSC	National Security Council
NSS	National Security Strategy
OBOR	One Belt One Road
PCA	Permanent Court of Arbitration
PLAN	People's Liberation Army (Navy)
PSI	Proliferation Security Initiative
ReCAAP	Regional Cooperation Agreement on Combating Piracy and Armed Robbery against Ships in Asia
RMA	Revolution in Military Affairs
ROE	Rules of Engagement
ROK	Republic of Korea
RTN	Royal Thai Navy
SAR	Search and Rescue
SCS	South China Sea
SIAC	Singapore International Arbitration Centre
SIASJ	Situations in Areas Surrounding Japan
SLOC	Sea Lines of Communication
SOP	Standard Operating Procedure
TsOR	Terms of Reference
UAV	Unmanned Aerial Vehicles
UNCLOS	United Nations Convention on the Law of the Sea
UNFCCC	United Nations Framework Convention on Climate Change
UNPKO	United Nations Peace Keeping Operations
VLCC	Very Large Crude Carriers
WFQR	Western Fleet Quick Response
WPNS	Western Pacific Naval Symposium

Contributors

First Admiral Amarulla Octavian
Chief of Staff, Western Fleet Command, Indonesian Navy

Rear Admiral Antoine Beaussant
ALINDIEN, French Navy

Vice Admiral Anup Singh (Retd)
Former Commander-in-Chief, Eastern Naval Command, Indian Navy

Prof Ataur Rahman
Chairman, Initiative for Strategic and Maritime Studies, Dhaka

Lt General Dan Leaf (Retd)
Director, Daniel K Inoyue Asia-Pacific Centre for Security Studies, Hawaii

Prof Eichii Katahara
Director, National Institute for Defense Studies, Tokyo

Prof Geoffrey Till
Professor Emeritus, King's College, London

Rear Admiral James Goldrick (Retd)
Adjunct Fellow, Australian National University, Canberra

Rear Admiral Raja Menon (Retd)
Distinguished Fellow, National Maritime Foundation, New Delhi

Prof Renfrew Christie
Defence & Strategic Analyst, South Africa

Vice Admiral Satish Soni
Flag Officer Commanding-in-Chief, Eastern Naval Command, Indian Navy

Prof Ye Hailin
Director, Center for South Asia Studies, Chinese Academy of Social Sciences (CASS), Beijing

Introduction

The relationship between humans and the oceans extends as far as five millennia. It is also an accepted axiom that the seas have shaped human destiny since antiquity. There is strong element of continuity and in the contemporary world, the maritime domain offers a number of opportunities for economic and socio-cultural engagements.

In the twenty-first century, Asia is at the centre stage of the global economic, political and security discourse. The 'Rise of Asia' is largely attributed to the economic development as also to a greater geostrategic heft in its maritime configured rim comprising both established and emerging powers. While the rapid economic growth of the region has contributed to a strong interdependence within and beyond Asia, the regional security environment faces new challenges emerging from the changing power dynamics among states, ongoing maritime-territorial disputes and issues relating to the freedom of navigation and overflight, which have become sharper. There are also visible anxieties related to the regional naval modernisation programmes. However, nontraditional security threats and challenges have encouraged institutional mechanisms towards a cooperative management of the sea areas for a safe and secure environment. In this milieu, the navies continue to make a seminal contribution to peace and stability at regional and global levels, which transcend the narrow national interests. It was with this background that the theme of 'Partnering Together for a Secure Maritime Future' was devised for the two-day international conference held during the International Fleet Review 2016 (IFR 16) at Visakhapatnam.

This edited volume is a compilation of papers and presentations made during the conference and comprises two broad sections. The first section examines the subject of 'Importance of Oceans and Navies in the Global Geostrategic Matrix' and within this, four issues have been debated and discussed:

- Trends in the growth of maritime military power
- Imperatives for building a balanced forced structure and balanced ends-ways-means for transnational and state-centric challenges

- Institutional linkages for enhancing maritime security cooperation
- Maritime capacity building and capability enhancements

At another level, significant changes are at play in the oceanic domain and are being driven by cooperative and competitive discourses with the traditional and new maritime players, realigning their posture within this somewhat uncertain environment. A number of countries have announced new naval strategies or maritime policies while others are engaged in revising and refining their current approaches to the naval and maritime developments. Although cooperation and competition are inherent in any relationship, it is the mechanics of competition management and enhancing cooperative agenda that is likely to shape the future of the world's oldest commons. The current trends acknowledge that cooperation is the key to secure the seas for the flow of global trade and for disrupting the motives of non-state actors. The focus is on acquiring the capacity as well as the capabilities for overall economic development and social prosperity. The second section of this volume is on the sub-theme of 'Regional Perceptions and Approaches for Maritime Cooperative Engagements' and covers:

- Managing competition in an uncertain but increasingly globalised oceanic commons
- Frameworks for enhancing interoperability at sea
- Maritime domain awareness as a tool for naval cooperation
- Relevance of existing international frameworks for conciliation and arbitration as a resolution mechanism.

The book concludes with a 'Tour de Horizon' based on the valedictory address where the larger arguments made during the Conference are summated.

The editors acknowledge the overall support provided by the IFR Cell, not only for coordinating many issues associated with the Conference but also for the publication of this volume. The valuable assistance by the Maritime Warfare Centre, Visakhapatnam [MWC(V)] for conducting the event is noteworthy. The editors would also like to recognise the contribution made by Ms Nitika Srivastava and Ms Premesha Saha, Research Associates at the National Maritime Foundation, for their diligence during the preparation of this volume.

Vijay Sakhuja
Raghavendra Mishra

Section I

Importance of Oceans and Navies in the Global Geostrategic Matrix

1. No Way But the "Hi" Way

Anup Singh

War has been described as a state of armed conflict between societies, generally characterised by extreme collective aggression, destruction and usually, high mortality. The absence of war is described as a state of 'peace'. According to Henderson, between 3500 BC and the twentieth century, a total of 14,500 wars have been fought by humanity and the toll has been a massive 3.5 billion lives. However, more alarming is the fact that out of these 5500 years, only 300 years were of peace on this planet.[1] Nevertheless, amongst all the wars therein, the most devastating of all has been the Second World War, with upwards of 65 million deaths. Without doubt, the winner in all post-modern wars has been the arms bazaar.

It was after the Second World War that the world resolved to rectify all ills related to dispute and conflict by creating what seemed to be a utopian establishment in the form of the United Nations. Comfort in this thought was short lived as a completely new form of stress took over international relations, within two years of the end of World War II: the Cold War beginning in 1947. Moreover, when the Cold War ended with the fall of the Berlin Wall in 1989, all nations anxiously awaited the dawn of the much-announced *new world order*. What the world has turned out to be instead is in some ways worse than during the Cold War. The spectre of conflict—both localised as well as 'regional'—is being fuelled by intimidation, disputes over sovereignty, sectarian violence and challenges posed by transnational crime across the seas. This mix of threats and challenges does not augur well for a peaceful coexistence and sustainable economic development of nations.

Maritime Security

Preamble

At the outset, it must be clearly understood that when it comes to maritime security anywhere in the world, the layperson cares little about the subject. To the common man, security in the maritime domain is of little relevance, and he would rather pay attention to something more 'earthly', 'commonplace' and 'interesting'. This is because man is basically a continental creature, and tends to take only matters related to *terra firma* seriously. It does not matter if the oceans constitute 71% of planet earth; it does not matter if most of the global economy was dependent on the carriage of merchandise over the medium of water. To a human being, the limits of life's activities are defined by his/her own boundaries—unless a person is venturing into the sea for economic or leisure activity (of which there are a miniscule few—including the seamen who man the 100,000 odd seagoing vessels of the world). But, one must appreciate that 85% of the world's goods by volume and 75% by value, have no alternative but to take the sea route. This is because the sea connects the world without barriers of territory, terrain, or toll, and ships offer the cheapest mode of transportation of bulk goods. With this scenario being a 'given', all national and global economies are heavily (almost entirely) dependent on the sea. Any disruption or threat of disruption will entail heavy penalties to the concerned economies (including the landlocked ones).

Types of Threats at Sea

Traditionally, there have been two types of threats from the sea. The first is the threat to shipping or sea lines of communication (SLOCs), and the second is the age-old threat to territorial integrity, which takes the form of surreptitious or overt conquest. It is to keep these traditional threats at bay, that maritime nations have always had navies as defenders of the vital maritime interests of their nations.

However, the situation at sea has undergone a huge change since the fall of the Berlin Wall. After the end of the Cold War, some ancient and some new types of non-traditional threats have taken root in some regions—notably the Indo-Pacific, where these seem to have assumed prominence, side-stepping the traditional forms of threats. It appears as if many suppressed challenges were unleashed for assault through the sea route, or otherwise. These are now being encountered by many maritime states. The actors of these threats may be states or 'non-state' in character. Most examples of transnational crime are found within the package of non-traditional threats. These include maritime terrorism, drug smuggling, gunrunning, human trafficking, human smuggling, piracy and armed robbery. Even manmade or natural disasters are threats of huge magnitude that keep the maritime forces engaged in the task of providing humanitarian assistance and disaster relief (HADR)—a prominent function of maritime forces today. These nontraditional threats were always 'listed' in the book and practised in some regions,but on a very small scale, and were faced only as isolated cases until the early nineties. Today however, it is these nontraditional challenges that constitute a majority of the threats to peace and good order in the medium of the seas—the most important of the global commons.

The world is also witnessing the re-emergence of the Cold War example of deliberate intrusion by extra-regional powers. This takes the form of "presence" missions in other regions by ambitious and emerging maritime powers. Such presence is seen as attempts by outsiders to exercise power projection, and makes the resident states most uncomfortable. A continued incidence of such presence requires an adequate response in marking and shadowing by the resident littorals for their own defence. It breaks the equation of mutual trust and only stretches the national security effort. This new form of challenge can be termed as 'neo-traditional'.

The terrorist attack on the USS Cole in the Aden harbour in the year 2000, on MV Limburg in 2002 and the Mumbai attacks in November 2008 are examples of transnational maritime terrorism which affect all nations and their security calculus. Similarly, piracy in the Straits of Malacca and the Gulf of Aden affects the global economy through enhanced costs of merchandise traffic and provision of additional security measures by the Flag States. The malaise of gunrunning and its nexus with drug smuggling across the 'hash highways' of the Indo-Pacific poses that type of threat to the national securities which requires enhanced patrolling by the maritime forces.

Sea Governance

Remedial Measures

All the challenges listed above can be pre-empted and neutralised more effectively if, instead of any independent action by the individual nations, the following measures are adopted by all the maritime states:

- Create a 'Balanced Fleet' with a force architecture that offers the flexibility to tackle all situations—traditional, nontraditional, and neo-traditional—in the most effective and economical (efficient) manner. What can be achieved by offshore patrol vessels (OPVs) should not be tackled with expensive frigates and destroyers.
- Encourage mechanisms of coordinated action by maritime neighbours to tackle transnational crime. The success of India–Myanmar, India–Indonesia, and India–Thailand coordinated patrols (CORPATS) is an apt example for emulation in all regions. This way, while an assemblage of force provides the needed heft against a challenge, the combined effort also enhances trust and interoperability amongst the stakeholder nations.

Freedom of the Seas

In recent times, 'freedom of the seas' as a phrase has received common usage amongst maritime states and their navies due to the many instances of disputed claims pertaining to major parts of the maritime zones or features. These disputes have led to one side or the other (or both) claiming jurisdiction over parts of the ocean that were not theirs. In some cases, these claims have also led to restrictions on the innocent passage for shipping. This is where the Law of the Sea is violated. Such unilateralism needs to be arrested and the existing fiats rectified.

History of Debate: The Free Sea

While the above disputes are of recent origin, the issue of freedom of navigation predates even the customary maritime law. It has been contested and fought for since ancient times. For example, the Mediterranean Sea saw itself being occupied and controlled by one entity—the Roman Empire—from about 30 BCE till 117 CE. The Romans named the seas as *Mare Nostrum* (Latin for 'our sea').[2] Until then, the ocean was never seen as 'territorial'. Further, in those days, the weather in the Mediterranean was found to be the most inhospitable for the type of vessels then in vogue during the period form November to March. So, a new term *Mare Clausum* (closed sea) came into use for the first-time ever.[3] However, this term was not seen as pejorative or as an enforcer of state jurisdiction as much as the first term. *Mare Clausum* was pronounced for the safety of shipping during the bad season. Later, in the middle ages, states like the Republic of Genoa and the Republic of Venice claimed a 'closed sea' policy, leading to the *Mare Clausum* being seen as an aggressive, self-proclaimed law. Portugal and Spain were most prominent in claiming exclusive rights over new lands discovered by them and the sea areas surrounding those lands. More of this was witnessed in the British waters in the following centuries. It was under these circumstances that Hugo Grotius, the famed Dutch jurist, propounded the theory that the sea was 'international' in nature and was free for all nations to use. His famous book, *Mare Liberum* (The Free Sea) published in 1609, demanded an end to the practice of the ownership of the seas and insisted that the oceans were a common medium for enabling trade and travel for all nations of the world.[4] Not to be outdone, Sir John Selden, a famous British jurist and historian, wrote his treatise *Mare Clausum* in 1635.[5] His was an attempt to legitimise the British claims to sovereignty over the waters around the British Isles and to further the British ambitions of dominating world trade. It is since then that the larger world community began its struggle to secure a set of rules aligned with the thesis propounded by Grotius, to eliminate competition between the 'haves' and make the seas a peaceful territory—common for the use of all nations.

Law of the Sea

Following the Truman Proclamation of 1945 declaring jurisdiction over the Continental Shelf,[6] a season of competition and disputes ensued and the international community found reason to seek a codified set of rules to 'govern' and create conditions for good order at sea. Thus was born the Third UN Conference for the Law of the Sea. Hailed as one of the greatest international achievements of the last century, the successful conclusion and subsequent coming-into-force of the convention that resulted from this conference—the Third United Nations Convention on the Law of the Sea, 1982 (UNCLOS III)—was seen as the ultimate panacea for all conflict related to contradictory claims and unilateralism. It was considered as 'one of the greatest' because it dealt with a most contentious subject of establishing rules for the maritime commons including the establishment of maritime zones. Indeed, this was no mean achievement as it cleared the many ambiguities leading to inequities amongst the maritime nations and many a conflict over the centuries. The debate on the freedom of the seas was finally 'settled' through an overwhelming consensus.

Post-UNCLOS Disputes

Despite being hailed as one of the most successful agreement among states, the Convention has not been able to prevent new disputes from emerging. In some cases, such disputes have had some historical background and are somewhat understandable; but, it is those that have erupted suddenly—well after the coming-in-to-force of the UNCLOS—which are now creating a Cold War-like situation. The Indo-Pacific region in particular, takes a majority of the blame for these disputes that threaten peace therein.

One would have thought that instances like the 'Cod War' should have been consigned to history as an example of anarchy in the absence of 'governance' before UNCLOS III. However, the many disputes that have arisen after 1982 raise the question of the effectiveness of the UNCLOS as an instrument to ensure equitable distribution.

One of the primary reasons for these disputes is the lure of potential riches that can be harvested from the seas, apart from the expansion of jurisdiction over water. Overlapping claims at sea are as contentious as territorial disputes on land. At times, these have been seen to be even more contentious than their mainland examples because of mineral resources—particularly hydrocarbons. Take for example the conflicting claims in the South China Sea where China and five other countries claim some or all of its islands, rocks and waters. China has, over the years, started asserting a claim of this sea being its 'own waters'. In some instances, it has challenged others' right even to the freedom of navigation. However, the primary reasons for its claims are: first, the right to exploration for what may be enormous reserves of hydrocarbons, making that sea such a 'gold mine'. Second, some of the artificial islands under reclamation in that water body are being seen by others as being intended for serving as military outposts. The entire area—almost 90% of the South China Sea—falls within the 'Nine-Dashed Line' promulgated by China. An estimated 50% of the global shipping carrying goods worth US $5.3 trillion passes through the Indonesian Straits annually, and thence through the South China Sea. According to one Chinese estimate, possible oil reserves in the area are as high as 213 billion barrels. Estimates by the Energy Information Administration (EIA) of the United States put the proven reserves at 28 billion barrels which itself is a huge figure. Similarly, natural gas reserves are estimated at 900 trillion cubic feet (25 trillion cubic metres).[7]

The Chinese base their claims to the Nine-Dashed Line on the 'South Sea Islands Location Map' which was released by the (pre-Communist era) Chinese Government in February 1948. They say that ancient Chinese mariners had discovered the Nansha (Spratlys) Islands as early as the second century BCE, and that almost all features in the water body belong to China. The moot point, however, is how come these claims are not being annulled by any international body and why China never staked claim at the time of its first delimitation exercise? The UNCLOS cannot deal with such disputes. On the other hand, China has made it clear that it will settle disputes only bilaterally with individual claimants and neither multilaterally nor through international mediation.

Dispute Resolution

The increasing incidence of sovereignty disputes has now assumed alarming proportions. To resolve such disputes, only customary international law can be applied which may have been templated out of judgements for territorial disputes delivered by international courts and tribunals over time. Though sovereignty disputes can be subjected to third-party dispute settlement through a consent of the disputing parties, given the sensitivities associated with disputes like those in the South China Sea, it is unlikely that these can easily be resolved through third-party settlement.

It is widely believed that one of the most viable interim solutions in maritime disputes is for the claimants to set aside sovereignty disputes for the time being and jointly develop (exploit) the natural resources. Such agreements can take the form of provisional arrangements of a practical nature, as called for in Articles 74 and 83 of UNCLOS III.[8]

The UNCLOS makes a provision for the fact that it may be extremely difficult for States to reach agreements on maritime delimitation in areas of overlapping EEZ and continental shelf claims, and it purports to provide a temporary solution to this situation in paragraph 3 of Article 74 and Article 83.2. However, there are obligations contained in these articles that require the disputing states to make every effort to enter into provisional arrangements of a practical nature and, during the transitional period, without any prejudice to the final delimitation. Should such an attempt be made in the South China Sea? Why not? However, will the larger claimant agree? Well, there is no harm in trying when nothing else seems to work. What about the arbitration case filed by the Philippines in the Permanent Court of Arbitration? The process of law can carry on simultaneously. The most successful way of establishing peace in any situation is a dialogue with propositions that can satisfy disputants in the interim, if not permanently.

Future Trajectory

While cooperating to manage and exploit shared resources may be a preferred route for settling the overlapping maritime claims (rather than wait for long before an agreement to divide is made), the conditions necessary for such an arrangement to be decided upon are sometimes viewed as utopian. These include trust amongst claimants and the political will to withstand the domestic politics and changes in government. While fishing may be easy to divide, exploration and subsequent exploitation of resources like oil and gas normally have a timetable measured in decades. Joint agreements for such purposes will therefore have to provide for a continuity and stability far beyond the likely tenure of the governments that enter into such an arrangement. Disputes in the South China Sea have become potent symbols of nationalism for the citizens of the claimant states. It is therefore understandable that such an arrangement is not easily negotiable. Though entering into a joint development arrangement is the second-best option to having a defined maritime boundary, it is significantly less attractive than the preferred option of having exclusive rights to a defined maritime boundary. Therefore it is natural that the contesting states which may have agreed to a joint development arrangement, will wish to maintain their respective legal positions. Also, joint development arrangements are provisional arrangements—without prejudice to the final delimitation. The question that arises is: what is the way out of the series of imbroglios that seem to only multiply with each passing year? Joint development has worked in many cases, and avenues like the ASEAN Regional Forum (ARF), which have a wide base, must initiate the process of getting all parties on the table through Track 2 through forums like the Council for Security in Asia-Pacific (CSCAP) and ultimately graduate towards Track 1. ARF is one of those few regional organisations, which enjoy a large base of participant countries and can effectively carry forward work from Tracks 2 and 1.5, to Track 1. Apprehensions on one disputant sticking to the principle of bilateralism should not keep us from attempting Preventive Diplomacy.

Another action for the long term should be to start the process of review and renewal of UNCLOS III. Perhaps it is time to initiate an UNCLOS IV that must include a degree of predictability and dependability on the rules therein. With respect to maritime claims of the nature being seen, UNCLOS III sets forth the objective to achieve maritime delimitation but falls short in enunciating the principles and final methods for achieving equitable results. As maritime delimitation cases differ, consideration in the new Convention must be given to factors including geography, historical linkages and predictability in the affairs of states. Otherwise, disputes will not be restricted to the South China Sea alone; the Arctic and Southern Oceans may be the next hotbeds of contested claims! The casualties in such cases are not just victim nations and their sovereign rights, but the global economy (through threatened shipping), the fishing community, and the good order at sea.

The Arms Race

By definition, the term "arms race" implies an increase in the potential strength of the tools of military power by rivals in peacetime. While the term took root when France and Russia tried to outdo Britain's naval superiority in the late nineteenth century, the most vivid example of an arms race beyond State vs State and beyond a single region, was provided by the Cold War period when tension between the two sides gave rise to an era of 'quid pro quos' in terms of military capabilities. Such was the spontaneity of acquisitions (of military capability) that despite the existence of secrecy between the two blocs, the intelligence of new capabilities by one side gave reason to the other to supersede the adversary by acquiring an equal or greater capability.

After the Cold War, the most conspicuous case of an arms race was witnessed in West Asia, in the immediate aftermath of the Gulf War. The reason then was the fear of conquest by an over-powerful neighbour as demonstrated by Iraq over Kuwait. Another reason was the realisation that the capability to defend oneself in the event of a regional conflict in the Gulf was inadequate.

It is a well-known fact from history that "dominant" regional powers that rely too heavily on coercion instead of consensus in their interactions with other countries of the region, actually end up fuelling an arms race, apart from making others find counterweights by forging alliances and security pacts with outside forces. The Indo-Pacific is witnessing such a situation today. The unprecedented growth of one power's military capability coupled with its actions against neighbours and at sea, has given immediate reason for others to spend more on their respective militaries in order to improve their capability to adequately defend themselves in any conflict. Such a race is intended to bring about a balance of military power. As Charles H. Fairbanks says,[9] ".....the strange result is that the activity of the other side, and not one's own resources, plans, and motives, becomes the determinant of one's own behaviour." Analyses of many examples of arms race since the late nineteenth century have demonstrated that the likelihood of war increases as the accumulation of arms proceeds as part of an unnecessary competition. Generally, political purposes drive and govern an arms race. The situation being witnessed in the eastern Indo-Pacific is somewhat similar to the Cold War era. The growing military prowess of one power on the back of its impressive economic progress, coupled with a very aggressive attitude and assertive behaviour, is fuelling an unprecedented arms race in that region. This arms race is taking a toll on social development as the cost of investment in instruments like submarines and aircraft leads to a heavy diversion of scarce financial resources in the developing countries. Does the region need that kind of military hardware due to an unhealthy competition? Not really. What kind of prognosis can be derived from the prevailing situation? Evidence from the arms races of the past has revealed that sometimes they exacerbate a sense of rivalry, occasionally even determined the timing of a war! However, analyses have also shown that most often, a race also ends in a political settlement between rivals or in a decision by one side to moderate its build-up.[10] Sir Edward Grey's memoirs point at the origins of the First World War where he avers:

> The moral is obvious: it is that great armaments lead inevitably to war. If there are armaments on one side there must be armaments on other sides. While one nation arms, other nations cannot tempt it to aggression by remaining defenceless. Armaments must have equipment... each measure taken by one nation is noted and leads to countermeasures by others.

The thesis that the arms race was the primary cause of war became popular after the First World War, and powerfully shaped public opinion in the democracies that were reluctant to rearm against the Axis powers. It became an example of learning the wrong lesson from history. No arms race played a part in the origins of the Second World War; it was rather an insufficiency of armaments on the Western side that expedited the launch of assaults at such speed. One thing is therefore clear: an arms race cannot always be avoided, and if it can bring to bear deterrence on each side, it may actually turn out to be a balancer of power.

So, is the current arms race in the Indo-Pacific a good thing for economic progress and the strategic power of nations? Certainly not! This is because, firstly, there is a vast disparity in the military capabilities of the various countries that may defy the possibility of balance. Secondly, it will lead to an unending spree to spend and milk away financial resources from the limited kitty at the disposal of the developing countries. What therefore, is the answer to prevent an arms race that is clearly unproductive in the region? The answer lies in bringing all parties to the table in order to initiate dialogue and establish confidence-building measures (CBMs) through mechanisms that will engender mutual trust and bonhomie. Efforts by members of the Western Pacific Naval Symposium (WPNS) during the organisation's 2014 meeting, in agreeing to a mechanism entitled the Code for Unplanned Encounters at Sea (CUES), constitute a conspicuous baby step. More must follow in order to instill confidence amongst all stakeholders.

The Way Forward

The choice lies between good order and continued chaos at sea. A mature, post-war comity of nations that is already tired of nontraditional threats, would certainly opt for the former. The way forward for creating conditions that are conducive to peace, tranquillity and trust, is to create interfaces between the existing multilateral forums—both political as well as military—in a manner that such organisations talk to each other, exchange information and suggestions, and act to pre-empt the conflicting situations.

The first principle towards forging trust amongst maritime forces and their nations is through regular bilateral exercises, which should graduate to the multilateral format. Thus, the biennial 'MILAN' series held at Port Blair, Andaman Islands in India, the Southeast Asia Cooperation and Training (SEACAT) exercise, the Rim of Pacific Exercise (RIMPAC), Exercise Cobra Gold, etc., must feed in to respective regional naval forums like the WPNS and the Indian Ocean Naval Symposium (IONS) which in turn could draw linkages with regional politico-economic organisations like the Indian Ocean Regional Association (IORA), ARF, and even APEC, etc. Track 2 platforms could be equal partners in this endeavour. Efforts towards harmonising endeavours will surely yield some results that will breed mutual understanding. If these suggestions sound utopian, one should only look at some path-breaking examples of joint development of disputed sea areas between otherwise 'warring' maritime neighbours in some regions. If that can work, peacemaking mechanisms can certainly work as well.

With regard to the neo-traditional challenge of the day, emerging maritime powers must understand that the template of the Cold War era cannot be applied to the regions beyond home. No littoral in any region feels comfortable with the presence of extra-regional powers in its waters. The only exception is a legitimate presence (generally temporary) for situations requiring a multinational effort to ward of transnational crime or for peacekeeping under the aegis of the United Nations. Here again, the best way is to win (and keep) friends by establishing mutual trust through confidence-building measures that guarantee respect for non-interference in each other's maritime domain.

Since the end of the Cold War, the world has witnessed a gradual lowering of the threshold for the maintenance of peace, and the high cost of managing conflict. No one nation is happy with the current state of security in the oceans. All ills of the present day can be neutralised through mutual trust. Cooperation must become the mantra of the maritime nations, in order for them to be able to fight evil together.

Notes

1. Henderson, Conway W. *Understanding International Law*. Chichester, West Sussex, U.K.: Wiley-Blackwell, 2010, p. 212.
2. See, Tellegen-Couperus, O. E. *A Short History of Roman Law*. London: Routledge, 1993.
3. Ibid, p.32.
4. Grotius, Hugo, David Armitage, William Welwood, and Richard Hakluyt. *Free Sea*. Liberty Fund, 2004.
5. Selden, John. *Mare Clausum: The Right and Dominion of the Sea ...* London: Printed for Andrew Kembe and Edward Thomas, 1663.
6. President Truman made the famous proclamation in Sep 1945, declaring jurisdiction over resources of the continental shelf. It meant that the US had exclusive rights to all the natural resources of the subsoil and the seabed of the entire continental shelf of the country.
7. "South China Sea Issue Explained", - China.org.cn, http://www.china.org.cn/china/2012-07/18/content_25941294.htm.
8. Bernard, Leonardo. "Prospect for Joint Development of Hydrocarbon Resources in the South China Sea", http://csis.org/files/attachments/130606_Bernard_ConferencePaper.pdf.

9. Franks, Charles H. "Arms Race: The Metaphor and the Facts", *The National Interest*, Fall 1985, p. 77.
10. "Arms Race Analysis" by History Channel, Accessed January 12, 2016. http://www.history.com/topics/cold-war/arms-race.

2. Importance of Ocean and Navies in the Global Geostrategic Matrix

Dan 'Fig' Leaf

The world may appear like a family, but the existence of frictions, conflicts and occasional violence cannot be completely discarded. Also, the world has changed from the times of the Cold War, where confrontation was the norm and the dangers of a nuclear holocaust seemed very real. In fact, it has moved beyond that to a globalised, interconnected, interdependent order, where the conduct of States should be different and conflict avoided. It is possible to look beyond historical narratives for letting a fruitful and healthy relation to evolve between countries.

It is equally important to understand how this was achieved and the reality of the relationships in terms of their evolution. This is applicable to many relationships and conflicts in the Indo-Asia Pacific where the need should be to concentrate more on the future and not on the past. In the Indo Asia Pacific, the challenges posed by issues such as those posed by North Korea, the East China Sea and the South China Sea disputes, Russia's role, rising China, Kashmir, terrorism—to name a few—remain of concern to all. However, the region is also witness to an overall positive future trajectory. The changes in military partnership between Japan and Korea and Prime Minister Modi's outreaches are pointers; while these do not fix everything, they do show a positive focus on the future. Likewise, the US–Vietnam relationship is a good example. Thus, every relationship such as between China and Pakistan should be seen through this prism and much more emphasis be placed on the strategic intents.

In this new world, the navies as well as the air forces, share the same domain, perform the functions of allowing and denying access, and do this with discipline knowing that their operating strategic environment is harsh. The navies of the modern world also appreciate that domination is a bygone idea and cooperation is the way to pursue national interests, even when there is competition. In this context, the key to maritime security cooperation begins with a training and practice in norms, standards, rules and laws, all of which are its foundation pillars. This needs to be applied in the realms of bilateral and multilateral cooperation as well.

Bilateral cooperation has been the norm for decades; whereas, multilateral cooperation though existent, was significantly less prominent and effective than it is at present. Multilateral cooperation has become the leading idea for discussions in the present context. It should transcend discourse and become the contemporary practice since each human being and by extension, each nation, exists in a shared environment. For instance, in the Pacific region, there are practices and opportunities being offered in responding to natural disasters.

Another issue of importance is the Shared Domain Awareness. While there have been many technical advances in the field of Shared Domain Awareness, the sharing of information and knowledge still remains difficult, technologically and—more importantly—philosophically. Technologically, systems are not always going to cooperate owing to their designs, and philosophically, countries may not want to share information. Therefore, in exercises and conferences, there is a compelling need to find ways to share information with the other relevant stakeholders. In terms of general awareness, the maritime and aviation domains have witnessed a convergence of sorts but an actual congruence as suggested by some regarding information exchange will remain difficult in the foreseeable future. This is because maritime and aviation domain architectures are not the same and are dictated by unique spatial and temporal characteristics; like, ships can remain in water for much longer than one can remain airborne. This mixed air-sea cooperative mechanism would persist given their dimensional ubiquities. It is also for emphasis that the United Nations cannot enforce the MDA on countries beyond what the global community is ready to accept as part of its common international responsibilities, which is dictated by the minimum acceptable denominators of unanimous consensus. What the countries will want and be willing to share with their partners, friends and allies is very specific.

A further key element is the role of the navies in the modern world. The navies need to clearly share and communicate their intent as unambiguously as possible. This may not be easy because of the lack of transparency in such communications, due to different strategic cultures and approaches which in many cases are driven by domestic and external conditions as well as contradictions. However, such constraints can be overcome. To cite a recent example, the US Secretary of Defense, Ashton Carter, has invested significant efforts in clearly portraying the national intent. His statements on the Freedom of Navigation (FON), specifically in the South China Sea, clearly bring out what the US is doing; how it is doing and why it is doing. There is no confrontational intent in his statements; instead, it is a clear statement of the US strategic intent regarding the South China Sea.

Communication at the tactical level is equally important in order to avoid misunderstandings, conflicts and incidents at sea. There is one key element that every navy should consider, that is its proficiency in the English language. English is the language of securing cooperation and communication. A navy that does not invest in being able to communicate in the English language tends to wastes whatever it invests in the advanced technologies as it cannot communicate on an equal basis. Therefore, a proficiency in the English language has strategic and tactical importance.

In a globalised interconnected world and in an attempt to bring about cooperation, and given the naval advancements taking place around the world, the issue of an arms race requires deliberate consideration. In this regard, another aspect that needs to be factored in is the importance being accorded to this particular issue. It is opined that the factor of 'arms race' is not as large as it is made to be because the navies in the modern world have and will continue to exert a moderating influence. Through their discipline and by their proficiency, the navies make conflict less likely. These become the 'standard setters' in a somewhat semi-anarchical (less jurisdictional) oceanic milieu and oppose the efforts of those seeking a 'non-rule based' society. If the militaries and navies that routinely operate in an international environment are properly trained, equipped and placed under appropriate discipline, it becomes obvious that conflicts can never be in the interest of a country. Navies should become 'standard setters' not just for their tactical excellence and military preparedness, but also in equal measure through an adherence to rules, procedures, norms and laws.

This is not to deny that there are frictions in this world and that disagreements exist on certain rules and norms. There are still some who believe that dominance of others through power is possible. However, if the US has learnt anything from the past, it is that this is not the case as the smallest can thwart the ambitions of the greatest nation. Therefore, in the present world, militaries are not seen as creating conflicts, but as deterring them and facilitating their resolution according to rules and norms. There are reasons for such optimism. The South China Sea dispute may appear as complex, convoluted, intractable and unsolvable, but recently in the Bay of Bengal region, long-standing major maritime/territorial disputes between India, Bangladesh and Myanmar were resolved through arbitration. In a similar vein, at the other end of the Indo-Pacific region, a very contentious dispute between Chile and Peru was resolved by approaching the International Court of Justice (ICJ). It is also proposed that the resoluteness of other players in the Indo-Asia Pacific region based on rules, laws and norms will make it inevitable for

China to follow the same path in the South China Sea because this is essential for it to succeed as a major global power. While China cannot be coerced – nor its conduct as an independent sovereign entity controlled – it will have to cooperate as a great power given the determination of the other players in the region to pursue a peaceful, stable and a rule-based order.

At this stage, an important point for reiteration is that despite all the tensions and conflicts that obtain in this region, confrontation has been avoided. Navies of the region have avoided miscalculations, misunderstandings and accidents. The consensual and inclusive worldview of the navies has found resonance in this part of the world and every encouragement should be afforded for the naval assets to be the 'standard setters' – a portrayal of strength in moderation and creating an environment that allows peace, stability and prosperity to prevail.

3. South China Sea Disputes: Perceptions and Misperceptions among the Players

Ye Hailin

During the last two years, although the South China Sea (SCS) environment has been tense, it was generally at controllable levels and did not witness any military-to-military confrontation. The various incidents at sea, between China and Vietnam or between China and the Philippines, were mainly between government law enforcement vessels or were of civilian character. Warships were employed for surveillance and signalling deterrent postures. On the diplomatic front, the stances of the involved states were seen to be hardening, although efforts to engage and negotiate through bilateral or multilateral mechanisms continued.

The reason for this 'struggling but not breaking up' situation in the SCS was in no small measure due to the significant strategic imbalance between the countries that were directly involved. At present, Vietnam and the Philippines do not consider a direct confrontation with China as a feasible option. More importantly, both China and the US with their advanced military capabilities consider the use of force in the SCS as a secondary option. It appears that countries with stronger military forces are more willing to compete with other parties by playing to their advantages in other fields like economics, with military forces being mainly used to reflect strong stance and resolute signalling.

During this two-year period, despite the limitations of power equations, the main issue emphasised by the involved parties is that the SCS dispute has not reached the levels which would compel them to consider using force to resolve the issue. The policy goals of different countries in the SCS remain limited and controlling the situation rather than realising the final policy goals still remains the basic starting point. The strategies adopted by them often provide considerable room for manoeuvre and the more assertive actions often occur only at the 'stalemate' stage. The primary purpose of such actions seems to one be of avoiding unintended escalation as against conflict prevention.

The countries involved, whether direct or indirect, in the SCS dispute perceived the so-called 'peaceful and stable' status quo sought through the 2002 Declaration on the Conduct of Parties in the South China Sea (DoC) as not yielding favourable results, at least when seen from their respective standpoints. All parties have interpreted the 2002 DoC and the politically aspirational 'Peace and Stability in the South China Sea' statement from nation-centric prisms by making selective (and expansive) interpretations about the impact of their own and others' actions on the environment. Vietnam believed that the positioning of the oil exploration platform by China was detrimental to the stability in the SCS; the Philippines perceives that the island reclamation project by China brought about a change in the status quo and the United States believes that all actions by China in the region were attempts at altering the existing balance. However, neither Vietnam nor the Philippines perceive that similar activities by them in the SCS were also responsible for a changed environment. In addition, the US did not admit that its continuous deployment of military forces in the SCS was influencing the existing situation in any manner. In sum, as far the issue of status quo in the SCS is concerned, each party believes that only the other party is undermining it, thus harming the stability and threatening the peace in the region, whereas its own actions were at the most, forced defensive actions.

Vietnam: Opportunistic Strategy Limited by Internal and External Environment

Vietnam has the largest number of features under dispute with China in the SCS. It occupies/controls the maximum number of maritime features in the SCS and consequentially seeks the largest maritime entitlements. Theoretically, Vietnam's posture should reflect the strongest opposition to China in the SCS. However, due to the constraining effects of its limited strength as well as the internal and external environment, it has always adopted a 'pendulum-like swing' posture on the SCS issue.

On the one hand, Vietnam possesses the strongest military force (including naval capabilities) among the Association of South East Asian Nations (ASEAN) countries; however, it is not of much relevance when compared with the military and naval potential of China. In the '3.14' skirmish during 1988, the Chinese Navy overwhelmed the Vietnamese Navy. This incident exemplified the then existing imbalance in the naval capabilities between China and Vietnam. In the current context, the naval power differential has widened and the Chinese Navy is quantitatively and qualitatively better. Such an advantage makes the possibility of use of force by Vietnam against China even more unlikely while competing for maritime interests. Vietnam's acquisition of submarines and combat aircraft from Russia is essentially aimed at improving its deterrent posture vis-à-vis China rather than their actual usage against China for gaining control over the islands, reefs and other maritime interests claimed by it.

On the other hand, since the 981 drill rig was deployed in the disputed Xisha waters (the Paracels) which are claimed both by Vietnam and China, Vietnam was compelled to take reactive measures in support of its assertions which in some ways was also intended for maintaining its image within the ASEAN. The counter-response by China also indicates that Vietnam did not have the requisite ability to seriously interfere with China's activities. More importantly for Vietnam, the domestic riots that occurred due to a sensationalised exaggeration of this incident exposed the vulnerabilities of its domestic political system and economic environment. While it may be surmised by some that the anti-China protests and demonstrations in Vietnam during mid-May 2014 were supported by a section of senior officials of the Vietnamese party and the government, the subsequent anti-government movement forced Vietnam to review its posture on the SCS dispute. The hype attached to the SCS issue did not yield any concrete results for Vietnam, but brought to fore the proposition that it could pay a heavy price arising out of a turbulent domestic political situation which could lead to a regime collapse. Therefore, since June 2014, the Party as well as the Vietnamese government have taken steps to reduce the simmering domestic political tension and initiated efforts to repair the damage to bilateral relations with China by reducing the confrontational hues over the SCS issue.

It is also pertinent to mention that the diplomatic resources available with Vietnam on the SCS issue are limited. As a country with the same social system as China, Vietnam is unlikely to become a key partner of the US in this region as the Party and government of Vietnam still harbour a serious mistrust of the US. Further, Vietnam is not a key influential member within the ASEAN. As for other powers outside the region, such as Russia, India and Japan, for Vietnam, they remain disparate geographic entities unable to provide any meaningful assistance for fixing existential problems. Except for Russia, the support provided by India and Japan is limited and would not make any substantial difference.

Due to the aforementioned factors and the resultant constraints, the Vietnamese stance apropos China on the SCS issue remains one of opportunism with two basic approaches being available to it. First, it may fuel an anti-China sentiment by cooperating with the Philippines in the ASEAN institutions in an attempt to bring a regional pressure on China. By this stratagem, Vietnam would aim for certain compromises by China out of its consideration for maintaining good relations with the ASEAN, or at least make it pay more attention to the Vietnamese position. Second,

Vietnam may leverage similar political philosophies in Vietnam and China, and use inter-party relations as the means to communicate with the latter on the SCS issue. Further, it may want to leverage the Chinese 'goodwill' since Beijing would not like to see any political turbulence or in a worst-case scenario, a regime change in Vietnam. The 'public opinion' within Vietnam could become the tool in its interactions with China, but such use would be controlled in at least two ways. The 'public opinion' argument may be used in a confrontational manner seeking self-restraint from China on the premise that such pressure could undermine its existing political architecture. However, the effectiveness of these approaches remains doubtful. Vietnam would not be in a position to guarantee the desired results and assured of consequences by implementing such a strategy, since much would depend on China's response, which may not be along the lines anticipated.

The Philippines: "Pawn" Strategy with the Intention to Intensify the Situation

After the unsuccessful efforts by the Philippines during the 2012 Huangyan Island (Scarborough Shoal/Reef) standoff, it realised the significant changes in Chinese strategy. China will no longer be bound by the oft-quoted principle of 'hiding capacities and bidding time', but 'will do something' as regards the SCS issue. Faced with this new strategic reality, it seems obvious to the Philippines that a military confrontation with China seems an unviable option given its suboptimal military maritime capabilities. Therefore, diplomatic and legal means remain the feasible response options for the Philippines against China's new approach to the SCS dispute. The fundamental objective of its strategy would be to form a network with other like-minded countries and obtain as much support as possible from the international community. Based on this strategic logic, the Philippines could be termed as the only stakeholder in the SCS imbroglio, with direct or implicit stakes, which would be the least interested in an effective resolution or de-escalation of tensions in the SCS. It is surmised that in the case of a continuous worsening of the SCS environment, the international community, especially the Western countries, would transform their anti-China stance into support for the Philippines.

The only feasible option for Manila has obvious flaws in the implementation process. The Philippines has attempted a legal recourse to resolve the ownership issue of the disputed islands. Even if the final award of the ongoing international arbitration is favourable to the Philippines, it will not bring any changes in the control and administrative status of the disputed features. Further, China has been unequivocal in its stance of non-participation and non-acceptance of the ongoing arbitration process. The driver for the Philippines to initiate legal proceedings was that if China neither participates nor accepts the arbitration, then Manila stands to gain support from the larger international community and with inevitable damaging consequences to China's reputation and stature. In addition, such a posture for China will undermine its relationships with the near and extended maritime neighbourhood. This prospect is indeed possible, but will not result in the Philippines gaining any actual and concrete maritime entitlements.

It seems that the Philippines did not realise that the reason for China's refusal to participate in the arbitration was not guided by the consideration that the award might be unfavourable. A more important reason was that arbitration as a means of international intervention will not be acceptable to China—a country that is rising, increasing its strategic influence in regional affairs and is becoming increasingly confident. What China did not recognise was the possibility that the SCS may be dominated by other powers which intend to play a decisive role. The Philippines' increasing emphasis on legal means would lead to more emphatic diplomatic statements by China that its claims are compliant with the international law, a stronger rejection of intervention by the international court(s) and more robust assertions in support of its position. An intensification of tensions in the SCS would certainly enable the Philippines to gather attention or even a certain sympathy from the international community, but it would have to deal with an increasingly stronger China at sea. Unless China's pressure on the Philippines gets countered by a stronger power, the latter's strategy in the SCS does not appear to have made a rational calculation in measuring the consequential gains and reverses.

To summarise, the gaining of any international support by the Philippines with its below-par naval quotient and its status as a fringe player in the regional geopolitical landscape would be dictated by the attitude of other powers rather than the actions of Manila. In other words, it is only when the intended entity (the US) recognises the need to maintain a perpetual hostile stance against China that this public relations-centric approach of the Philippines would be effective. However, the US policy on China is apparently not being dictated by the SCS considerations alone.

The United States: Deterrence Intention and Control Strategy from Backstage to Forefront

Over the past year, the US stance on the SCS issue has become rigid, accompanied by a diplomatic pressure and an increase in the deterrent military activities. Such a shift was not accidental, but an inevitable result of the developments within the SCS and the likely future trajectory that the dispute might assume. The US is not a 'directly involved' party, but has always considered itself as the upholder of global maritime order including that in the SCS. Maintaining this global maritime hegemonic status by the US seems to be the core objective of the US maritime strategy. The US, undoubtedly a global leading power, may intervene and provide a special focus to certain maritime disputes at discrete locations, but has not shown the same interest in issues that do not impinge on its global maritime primacy such as the ones involving India and Bangladesh and India and Pakistan. This selectivity by the US stems not from the fact that these disputes impinge on its interests, but from the premise that such issues do not involve its global 'prestige'. With its relative decline, the US is likely to encounter more challenges and become more sensitive about its hegemonic status. In some measure, the increasing importance of the SCS issue in the diplomatic and military strategic postures could be correlated with a gradual decline of the US global dominance.

In a radical departure from the aims and aspirations of other countries such as Vietnam and the Philippines, the US is not much interested in the specific ownership of the islands and reefs under dispute in the SCS. The actual aim of the US is that it should be the sole 'rule-setter' and 'guarantor' of any eventual resolution in the SCS. Even if China was to reach a compromise with the related claimants on the SCS issue through diplomatic efforts involving significant concessions, the US will still not recognise such an arrangement as acceptable. What the US is really interested in is the issue of 'order' rather than 'result' which is evident from its attitude towards the 2002 DoC.

In 2002, China and the ASEAN countries reached a consensus over the DoC as a point of reference for resolution or at least as a consensual response mechanism to the SCS disputes. The American role in the formulation of the DoC was negligible since the US believed that this instrument would not upset its maritime hegemony, apparent in the initial years after the DoC finalisation. When the positive effects of the DoC started becoming apparent, the US was confronted with a serious situation. It was engaged in the 'Global War on Terrorism' in the Middle East and South Asia, its domestic economy had suffered a serious downturn, and its global prestige was at an all-time low—a period of transition from the Bush to Obama Administration.

All these developments made the US more sensitive about retaining its primacy in world politics. Since the latter part of the Bush Administration, the US started according a greater importance to the Southeast Asian region with obvious reservations about the joint efforts by China, the Philippines and Vietnam in managing the SCS issue. At this stage, the US believed that a de-escalation and even a final settlement of the SCS dispute without its active involvement was contrary to its interests. Therefore, with the beginning of the first Obama administration, the US actively advocated the 'Return to Southeast Asia' and 'Pivot or the Rebalance to Asia-Pacific' where the SCS issue became an important marker for its global leadership.

Further, the message of an ever-stronger 'American Century' could be delivered by stressing its leadership role, showcasing its military might and dissuading China from actions in support of its rights, including the construction activities in the SCS. The most appropriate situation that meets the US interests would be if its tactics were to compel China to seek an active US involvement in resolving the SCS dispute. As mentioned earlier, since the US is not a direct claimant, the rationale for its interference can be justified by maintaining the so-called international order by highlighting issues related to the freedom of navigation/ overflight and opposing the coercion of small countries by a bigger regional player. These two specific reasons have more to do with 'order' rather than the issue of a 'specific ownership' of the disputed maritime features. More importantly, the order perpetuated would be reflective of a US hegemony rather than the stability of the region or a successful settlement of the SCS issue.

However, the inherent problem of such an approach is that the American objective of maintaining its primacy will result in China selecting more confrontational strategies. In order to reflect its status, the protector of the order would raise specific issues and relate these to morality and justice, deny reasonable arguments by an involved party and interpret all the intentions/behaviour of one party as adversarial and subversive. From the US perspective, China's opposition to its interference posed a challenge to its 'global leadership'. Under such circumstances, the more the US stresses its right for maintaining the regional order, the more it will be rejected by China. As a result, the confrontation between China and US may increase. From Beijing's standpoint, the US intervention in SCS on the premise of maintaining 'order' is in effect another attempt to 'contain' China.

If the SCS issue were to be seen through a prism involving sovereignty/sovereign rights between China and the other direct claimants, the economic and politico-diplomatic costs through negotiation would be relatively low. However, as long as this issue is seen through a lens of 'order', it will make any compromises by either China or the US a sign of weakness which will only lead to a further hardening of the respective postures and confrontational attitudes. A reality that the US needs to understand today is that the possibilities of repeating its actions during the 1996 Taiwan Strait Crisis are low. Firstly, the power disparity between China and the US has obviously narrowed and secondly, the weak signalling by the US in response to other challenges makes China believe that the current administration is unwilling to enforce the hard-line policies of the Bush era. This reduces the effectiveness of the American deterrent actions in the SCS while encouraging China to develop tougher approaches in dealing with the other claimants.

However, it should also be considered that China and the US have engaged each other on many issues including the SCS, and developed a semblance of a crisis-control mechanism. However, these mechanisms work at a functional level with significant differences persisting on foundational aspects. The US intentions to force China in making a compromise under the ambit of international rules and rights written by it coupled with a diplomatic pressure will cause a further distrust in China, thus forcing the use of its strength at sea. Over the past year, the competition between China and the US on the SCS dispute can be characterised as an 'Oil-Adding Strategy'. The gradual hardening of stance by the US has met with Chinese resoluteness, with the confrontation intensifying between the two parties. The two main options for the US may be to take either a more nuanced mediator-cum-balancer role or increase its regional military capabilities as a deterrent against further actions by Beijing.

Opportunistic Others

As far as the members of the ASEAN and other involved countries outside the region are concerned, their policies and postures over the SCS issue can be categorised as opportunistic. The ASEAN does not want this issue to become the core subject affecting its relations with China. It also wants to avoid an internal split within this collective community. While ASEAN seems strongly motivated towards a reconciliatory approach, it has not been able to form a unanimous and coordinated stance vis-à-vis China. In addition, considering the overall positive relations between China and the ASEAN, and the favourable response to the 'Belt and Road Initiative' (BRI), it is unlikely that the ASEAN would be able to evolve a unanimous stance against China on the SCS issue. The articulations by the ASEAN during the ASEAN Defence Ministers Meeting Plus (ADMM Plus) Forum in April 2015 should be interpreted as its concern over the developments, and need not necessarily reflect that ASEAN wants to be an arbitrator or coordinator between China and the Philippines or Vietnam in settling the SCS dispute.

Japan's involvement in the SCS affairs has become more active. In the background of the China–Japan dispute and the increasing motivation to become a 'Normal Country', Japan has strong motives to participate in this dispute. On the other hand, it has differing interests in getting involved on this issue and its tougher stance is a reflection of its active strategy since a worsening of the SCS environment, which would deflect China from concentrating on the East China Sea (ECS) dispute. For Japan, the SCS dispute facilitates its aspirations of regaining the status of a political and military power in the world and complete the 'Normalization of Country'. However, owing to the contrarian influences being exerted by the domestic political landscape and the public opinion in Japan, it will take some time for the Abe government to transform this active stance on the SCS issue into actual actions.

For powers outside the region such as India, Australia, Russia and the European Union, their interests in the South China Sea are at their most marginal. Thus, their inputs are minimal without any significant impact.

China's Strategy Selection and the Direction of the South China Sea Issue in the Future

Although the South China Sea situation has been intensifying since early 2014, the policies of all the related parties are still evolving with continuous calibration. For China, the primary task in the SCS in 2014 was of capacity building with three linked aspects: to strengthen the functionalities of the Chinese controlled maritime features in the SCS and achieve the requisite power quotient for future military and law enforcement situations; a clear demonstration of China's posture, resolution and intent to protect its rights and interests in the SCS while opposing the US actions and promoting negotiations accompanied by pressure on the Philippines and Vietnam through strong maritime forces for these countries to discuss the SCS issue in a calm and rational manner.

China is not interested in a further intensification of the SCS environment, nor does it want to use this issue to subvert the current international order. A section of the Chinese analytical community interprets a deterioration of the SCS situation as a challenge and an obstacle to the successful implementation of its larger politico-diplomatic and other strategic policies, especially the BRI. The overall relations with the neighbouring countries, especially those of the ASEAN, still outweigh the maritime rights and interest issue obtaining in the SCS, which has obviously retrained China's actions. However, Beijing must remain mindful that such an approach should not provide an opportunity for the other claimants and stakeholders to put additional pressure on China.

To a certain extent, China's strategy can be interpreted as one of active control and of exerting a cost-imposing strategy through internal (hard) balancing.

This new strategical outlook has obvious advantages as compared with the previous passive control methodology being employed by China. Its ability to influence the direction of the SCS situation has improved significantly and its peripheral environment has improved, thus providing more options in the future. This position also comes with the caveat wherein the risk and possibilities of conflicts has also increased. In terms of the final direction of the Chinese strategy on the SCS issue, the advantages due to the improvements in its strategic capabilities are evidently greater than the superficial stability achieved through the passive compromise approach of yesteryears. The reactions of Vietnam, the Philippines and the US also prove the efficacy of this approach by China.

During this process of capacity building in the SCS, it is pertinent to mention that China does not perceive its actions as amounting to a change in the status quo as its activities were all implemented on the maritime features under its actual control. Further, China has not attempted to recover the maritime and territorial entitlements claimed by it but occupied/controlled by other countries. The argument that China's capacity-building efforts do not bring about a change in the extant balance, though obvious, has not been persuasive enough. China need not further reiterate this proposition and on the contrary, it should put more emphasis on the fact that these were reactions mandated after continuous efforts by other parties to alter the existing equilibrium in the SCS.

China's capacity-building exercise will inevitably call for the use of power in future. This issue will inevitably lead to further disputes with neighbouring countries. It is assessed that commencing with the second half of 2015 and from a near-term perspective, the subject of using military and civil facilities on the newly built and expanded islands and reefs in the SCS will gain a greater relevance. In this regard, China will need to accord particular attention to the southern part of the SCS considering the diplomatic and international discourse that may originate.

It is also opined that drawing an extensive extrapolation between the SCS environment and a successful implementation of the BRI strategy is neither mutually dependent nor contradictory. An early mitigation of the SCS situation is also not a precondition for the realisation of the BRI. The dominant player in the SCS is the US rather than the direct claimants and even if China were to make substantial compromises on the SCS disputes to promote its BRI strategy, the anticipated changes in the regional or even the international order brought about by this strategic outreach would not prevent the US from continuing with its obstructionist posture. This has been obvious in the preparatory processes of the Asian Infrastructure Investment Bank (AIIB). The SCS issue has indeed increased difficulties for China in obtaining support from the Southeast Asian countries regarding BRI. However, a favourable response to the BRI will not only depend on the strategic expectations of these countries but also will have to contend with the restraining effects of the US 'Rebalance to Asia-Pacific' strategy. Therefore, a positive fallout of the compromises on the SCS issue in garnering support from Southeast Asia for the BRI remains doubtful.

Conclusion

In the foreseeable future, the capacity-building efforts of China may lead to more tensions in the SCS. China would be cognisant of this trend and it is a path that it may have to traverse in order to transform its posture from that of 'creating an environment' to one of 'preserving the situation'. The length of this turbulent period will finally depend on the balance of power between China and the direct as well as indirect stakeholders in the SCS rather than their self-restraint.

4. Maritime Security and Navies: Future Challenges in the Indian Ocean

Antoine Beaussant

The importance of oceans and navies has a long lineage and in the twenty-first century brings at least three tipping points that merit attention.

First, the world has never been so blue; 70 per cent of the surface of the globe is liquid; 80 per cent of the world population lives less than 100 kilometres away from the seashore and 90 per cent of the commercial exchanges are done through the oceans.

Second, with the advent of law of the sea, which was universally recognised at the end of the last century, as well as with technological innovations, the use of navies at high seas has become an unavoidable asset in the strategy to develop power. The freedom of the seas is a tool (or a weapon) for the great powers since it is possible to get as close as 12 nautical miles from the coasts in compliance with the international law. Moreover, dissuasion and projection capabilities provided by the first-rank navies are decisive advantages for the policymakers. In this regard, aircraft carriers are said to be the 'best ambassadors'. It must, however, be added that technological advancements in submarines also contribute to the growing importance of navies, considering the inherent stealth, range of weapons and sensors as well as their ability to sustain for longer periods at sea. Therefore, underwater capabilities—in an equal measure—are key assets for covering the entire ambit from limited to credible deterrence.

Third, the international order is being restructured with the emergence of maritime powers, whose navies are advancing—especially in the Indian Ocean. An increase in the number of capable actors at sea is another significant change that needs acknowledgement. Half of the submarines in the world, it is believed, will belong to the Asian navies by 2030. Further, the sea which used to be considered a realm of freedom may become a lawless zone if the States do not cooperate and address the threat of anarchy at sea through improved multilateralism.

At this stage, it is considered pertinent to revisit the idea of the sea as an 'area of freedom'. Indeed, the challenge for States mainly lies in the effective management of the seas to take advantage of this relatively 'permissive zone' as much as possible, which in equal measure implies respecting the rights and interests of other States. The oceans are an area of diplomatic manoeuvre, which has not received due attention. Any State with an established political strategy should and must include a maritime component and take into account some key rules: the importance of dialogue, the necessary pooling of some capacities and the defence of common goods beyond nation-centric needs.

The use of naval diplomacy in order to influence regional matters was illustrated quite recently in the Gulf region. In April 2015, during the Yemen crisis, the Iranian deployment of commercial vessels and warships to supply a section of Yemenis in the Gulf of Aden had an impact on the American diplomatic posture even when Tehran eventually withdrew its assets due to the deterrent presence of the US Navy ships. This event showed how a navy could be a meaningful and effective politico-diplomatic card for the Americans as well as for the Iranians. This naval tool is all the more significant since it can be employed in a graduated manner, thereby enabling an adjustment of the 'ways and means' according to the desired effect. The deployment of naval assets, the interception of foreign-flagged vessels, or an exercise at sea with an aggressive scenario constitute some examples within a very large range of possibilities which obtain at sea.

To add, a near-constant presence of nuclear-capable maritime forces extending from the Indian Ocean to the Western Pacific would be a reality in the next 15 years and this would progressively change the regional balance of power. The period of transition towards postures of 'rational deterrence' will imply some inherent risks.

Thus, it is important to discuss strategic postures at every level to avoid miscalculating the intent of the other party. It is the same with regards to the management of interactions at sea between naval assets, whose number is ever increasing. At the tactical level, the development of codes for unexpected encounters at sea in the Pacific and in the Indian Ocean illustrates this new challenge of coordination.

Another challenge is about learning to work together, especially if the US presence is likely to reduce in the Indian Ocean in the years to come, because of the current rebalancing towards the Asia-Pacific region. At the recent Galle Dialogue, the articulations by representatives of different regional navies were a testimony that the implications of such a possibility are clearly understood. The situation is not very different in the Gulf, even if the American presence would remain important. The Gulf States are integrated within the Combined Maritime Forces (CMF) and they should be relied upon to play an increasing role in the region. The projected setting up of Task Force 81 comprising naval assets of the Gulf Cooperation Council (GCC) countries remains on track even if there is still a long way to go before it becomes a reality. In addition to this, there is also the necessity of budget sharing when mutual interests can be found, particularly for states whose navies remain the poor cousin of the armed forces.

Finally, the States and their aspirations can also jeopardise the freedom of the seas. The territorialisation of the seas seems to be inevitable in a world where resources are becoming increasingly limited. Without making nation-specific statements, a reference to some public statements about the Exclusive Economic Zones (EEZ), formulation of inconsistent (or excessive) baselines and expansive claims about continental-shelf entitlements can be made. Such areas of contentious overlap between neighbouring coastal states can be peacefully resolved through internationally prescribed means in the same manner as litigations ashore. However, the high seas' freedom is also threatened by the phenomenon of 'access denial' strategies that have found much discussion in the Pacific Ocean region. A collective defence of the freedom of the seas thus becomes a universal imperative as a common good which would require the global seafaring community to transcend the narrow boundaries of national interests.

This leads to another important issue which is about transnational challenges. The current globalised world needs to address the challenges posed by the increasing human activities. It is a global concern which brings to the fore the question of State responsibility for environmental conservation, a subject that lay at the core of the twenty-first meeting of the Conference of Parties (COP21) at Paris comprising 195 nations that make up the United Nations Framework on Climate Change (UNFCC). Towards this end, the seas have acquired a particular but recent relevance. It would be worth recalling the doctrine of the 'freedom of the seas' (*Mare Liberum*) as espoused by Hugo Grotius in the seventeenth century. His vision that has prevailed so far can be summarised through four propositions:

First, it was articulated that since the goods required for mankind are unequally distributed in the world and that by the law of nature, divine will dictates that nations may exchange and communicate with each other freely to meet their needs.

Second, as the oceans are designated by God to be the great road for such a reciprocal commerce between the nations, it implies that the oceans belong to all.

Third, what would be the point for a people in possessing vast seas, even if it were possible? The seas are like the air we breathe, unlimited in substance and in use. The sea can fulfil the needs of all of us, be it to navigate on its surface or fish in the deep.

Fourth, this property would be impossible to claim, impossible to encompass, impossible to defend. How could we take possession of waves and flows? Could it be possible to draw a permanent border on a liquid element?

These dictums are substantive issues for attention as these thoughts remind us of our collective responsibility. And as a naval practitioner, it would be correct to state that such a logic remains an innate part of a seafarer's genetic heritage.

The seas, collectively, are indeed an area of freedom and it is also evident that this freedom needs to be husbanded and cherished. However, as noted earlier, the seas might also become lawless zones, due to the increasing instances involving breaches of the public order ashore which could undermine the national maritime strategies. Thus, enhanced cooperation between navies is needed all the more to check the rising and the continual adaptation of criminality at sea.

In this regard, the first point for emphasis is about the roots of the problems that lie ashore and which result in situations at sea. These roots come from failed or fragile states which are fertile grounds for the development of illicit activities at sea. Beyond the different expressions of this criminality (piracy which is declining, other forms of organised crime at sea which are emerging or increasing), it is important to understand that the inextricable situations ashore have very serious consequences at sea.

An important trend that has been quite evident in the recent years is the rise of maritime insecurity in proportions that seem to have increased to historic levels in an era of general interstate peace. Maritime insecurity has its origins ashore and the its manifestations such as piracy, drug trafficking, weapon or migrant smuggling, terrorism at sea, etc., have their causes on land. When the situation deteriorates ashore and the public institutions cannot deliver governance and ensure public order leading to political instability, the populace of these affected regions or areas comes under pressure and is faced with closed borders; it then finds the only freedom zone to be the sea.

In a sense, this trend could be termed as a 'piston effect' where pressure forces people into migrating to a free zone; piracy off Somalia is its apt example.. Drug trafficking from Afghanistan is another, as well as the flow of migrants in the Mediterranean Sea (originating from Syria/Libya) and the Gulf of Guinea, etc. In this respect and in current context, the northern part of the Indian Ocean is particularly vulnerable; after Somalia, it seems to be the turn of Yemen to plunge into anarchy. It is important to mention that the Bab-el-Mandeb is now witnessing increasing pressure from these two anarchic territories for which the price will be paid at sea.

The rising insecurity at sea leads to another downside, which is the privatisation of safety at sea. While large-scale piracy has almost disappeared in the Indian Ocean, the quasi-legal market it has generated remains very lucrative. A large number of shipowners, as well as major energy conglomerates, have developed their own mechanisms for counter-piracy protection like the use of Unmanned Aerial Vehicles (UAV), embarked security teams, etc. The problem that such developments cerate are in myriad forms which include legal issues as well, thus adding another layer of 'force' afloat, thereby increasing the level of violence. It is opined that the use of force at sea must remain a State prerogative requiring adequate investments in credible military maritime capabilities.

The increasing insecurity at sea with different facets like pollution by ships is one of the major issues at stake. While violence at sea is not new, what is new is the scale of these phenomena and the possibilities of proliferating links between terrorism and international criminality by using the medium of the seas. Unlike the other forms of criminality against which efficient responses have been found, such as piracy, the States in the Indian Ocean (or elsewhere) do not seem to be prepared against maritime terrorist threats at sea. This originates from a lack of common understanding and inadequate attention, which can be seen from recent attacks despite serious warnings a few years ago. These threats have global connotations since they endanger vital national interests by striking at critical vulnerabilities. While there is a growing interest on the subject of Maritime Infrastructure Protection (MIP) which is of contemporary relevance, unfortunately it has not been implemented in a true operational sense so far by the global community.

To summarise, this zone of freedom today is coming under increasing pressures. It is being threatened by new and expanding sets of threats and challenges with the possibility of a virtual anarchy pervading across the maritime realm. In the absence of any sustained and close attention, the chances of losing this priceless legacy inherited from Grotius seem very real. The key question that demands an answer today is how to prevent this loss of the freedom of the seas resulting in widespread insecurity and the seas becoming a lawless zone? In response, two approaches can be stated.

The first option is of adopting a 'defend the fortress' philosophy with a coastal protection system with a multitude of sensors and technical devices against criminal elements including situations like distress at sea and pollution risk. However, such a system is not flawless as it is quite easy to find countermeasures to such a coastal protective wall—precisely because of the freedom of movement provided by the medium of the seas. It is an approach that will remain limited by national interests and to the jurisdictional zones of a coastal State, which eventually translates into a partial and insufficient response to a borderless threat. It is a defence based on technological solutions which could to be vulnerable to possible failures and asymmetric attacks.

The second option is of a 'deep, forward defence' based on a comprehensive coalition strategy that goes beyond a technology-focused and a nation-centric approach. This option of responding to contemporary and future challenges implies information and intelligence sharing, operational cooperation and a relevant legal framework to prevent a culture of impunity on the high seas by suitable modifications to the flag state provisions, in accordance with international law. Working together within the combined maritime task forces, with the working groups of the IONS, setting up exchange mechanisms for information and intelligence, etc., are all valuable functional mechanisms that need to be encouraged.

To conclude, it is important to understand the underlying intent contained in the profound words of Cardinal Richelieu, Prime Minister of France in the seventeenth century who used to aver that "the tears of our kings have the salty taste of the seas they ignored". The leadership of the nations that are and those that aspire to be maritime powers should make all the efforts for highlighting the importance of maritime issues at the policy levels, while also emphasising the critical need for a collective and global approach.

If a transformation of the 'freedom of the seas' into 'zones of freedom' for the criminals is to be prevented and if the important maritime stakeholder nations are willing to engage in a collaborative and anticipatory approach for synergistic actions against a danger occurring far away from its origins, the existing focus on a bilateral maritime cooperation would not be sufficient. In the face of an increased maritime criminality that is assuming an unforeseen networking which is both insidious and adaptable, a comprehensive multilateral approach becomes the only feasible solution. Collective and multipronged counter-piracy operations and their successful outcomes have proven that it is possible to work together. France remains committed to and seeks a similar approach to support a system of international maritime cooperation and sharing of information with the higher aim of obtaining collective operational responses at sea which should extend beyond the words stated at committees, symposiums and other dialogue forums.

5. Towards a New Maritime Strategy for Medium Powers: Defining the Challenges for the Medium Power Navy

James Goldrick

The Medium Maritime Power

What is a medium power? Richard Hill examined this question in detail in his 1986 book *Maritime Strategy for Medium Powers*. He assessed that superpowers are unlikely to suffer direct challenges to their territory, their political independence or their national welfare. Small powers, on the other hand, are unable to guard their own interests without some form of external support and guarantee. Medium powers fall between these two groups and are identified not so much by inherent characteristics as by their primary security objective. Hill suggested that a medium power seeks to 'create and keep under national control enough means of power to initiate and sustain coercive actions whose outcome will be the preservation of its vital interests'.[1]

It follows that a medium maritime power is one that has vital interests in the maritime domain and some capacity to protect them. This does not mean, however, that medium powers are capable of advancing every aspect of such vital interests by themselves. This is a key issue. As Hill has noted, "medium powers need to be as brave as lions and as cunning as foxes".[2] Each medium power needs to achieve a balance between national autonomy and cooperation or alliance with other nations, with an equivalent balance between its national capabilities and the extent to which its agencies will interact with those of the other nations to protect its interests.

Given that this goal spans the entire spectrum of conflict, it also follows that this is inherently a whole of government effort and will involve both civil and military elements. Furthermore, maritime air forces and amphibious land forces must be considered as integral to any assessment of the military requirements as navies. Effective joint and inter-agency intelligence and command and control systems are also essential force multipliers for any medium power and they must be joint and inter-agency without duplication.

Defining the Problem

Determining both the necessary overall commitment and the balance of government effort is not an easy task. Nevertheless, judgements can be made. The first is that nation-states, despite the progress of globalisation, will continue to be a principal factor in international relations. Coercion, the use of force or the threat of the use of force, will remain a feature—however undesirable—of their interaction. This reality is one that medium power governments need to bear firmly in mind when contemplating the future of armed conflict.[3]

The point is particularly acute for Western Europe. In the wake of the Cold War and the appearance of what many judged to be new, 'non-traditional' threats to international security, there was a tendency to assume that the 'modern' era of nation-states had come to an end, and that the 'post-modern' environment demanded very different approaches—ones in which the utility of military forces designed for state-on-state warfare was increasingly doubtful. There was certainly hard truth in the assessment that there were new challenges to be faced and new methods to adopt, but this judgement was never complete for the Indo-Pacific, in which the forces of nationalism remained and remain at play. Recent events in the Crimea and the Ukraine and Russian posturing have provided compelling evidence that, even if 'post-modernism' were applicable to Europe between 1992 and 2010, it is not so now.

All this has implications for the maritime environment and arguably, will force a rebalancing of many navies away—to an extent—from their recent focus on the projection of power ashore. The latter approach was logical when the West was supreme at sea following the end of the Cold War,[4] but is not enough when there is any possibility that control will once more be contested. The new reality may be much more like that of the Cold War itself, when naval forces had also to focus on protecting the shipping that supported both their national economies as well as the campaigns on land.[5]

Ironically, events of the last decade in the Indian Ocean have shown that such requirements for sea control have a non-state dimension as well. Although many navies will have to adapt to meet the re-emerging state-on-state situation, the challenge for maritime powers has been and remains one of complication and not substitution. Armed conflict is acquiring further dimensions; it is not losing them. To the rivalries of nation states must be added the activities of non-state organisations, such as terrorists and transnational criminals, as well as the consequences of economic, political and environmental failures. Practically, all these issues and problems have a maritime context, even in the e-environment. Piracy and armed robbery at sea continue to occur in the maritime domain wherever governance is weak and the targets are available.[6] A significant proportion of the increasing activity in illegal immigration is by seaborne means. Drug smuggling is another activity of international organised crime that has a significant (and probably growing) maritime element.[7] Environmental degradation is a fact of life and there is the prospect of increasing competition at sea for a greatly depleted and constantly diminishing amount of living natural resources.[8]

Medium powers and their agents will need to do more—not less—to adapt to all these situations. They will also need to do more—not less— to meet the spectrum of conflict, to 'orchestrate both hard and soft maritime power'.[9] Given the inherent constraints on resources which medium powers possess, this complicates their situation even further. To what extent do medium powers distribute their resources between high-level war-fighting capabilities and those required for other operations? How much should remain with physical 'kinetic' elements for the application of force and how much is to go to the emergent cyber-warfare systems? What will be the division of labour, and thus of resources, between navies and other maritime agencies in meeting all the threats to good order at sea?

The 'Revolution in Military Affairs' and the Relationship Between Conflict Intensity and Technology

The waters have been further muddied by technological developments. These create not only very significant problems but also potential opportunities. Extraordinary advances in command, control, communications, computers and intelligence, as well as surveillance and reconnaissance, make long-range precision weapons a key threat to forward deployed naval forces and also to those operating in the open ocean. The proliferation of unmanned systems, whether as sensors, weapons, or both, adds another complication. However, access to these same technologies may permit maritime forces to achieve much higher degrees of what is now being termed as 'battlespace awareness'[10] than has ever before been possible, conferring on them new powers of offence and defence. In future, surface ships may become hosts for their own above, on and underwater 'swarms' creating local networks that will act as defensive bubbles and which may be more robust than the dispersed systems ranged against them which depend upon remote intelligence and control. Manned submarines may also act as 'masters of the swarm' in similar ways, albeit utilising much more covert management techniques.

One important consideration for maritime operations is that the intensity of a conflict and the sophistication of the technology employed within that conflict do not have a direct relationship. Nor is there any certain relationship between warning time and the weapons that may be employed. This understanding needs to be a key consideration in the assessment of naval requirements. Missiles can be acquired and other elements of military capability readily assembled by those who have the funds and the will. The construction and use of small submersibles for drug smuggling is one example of this reality. The successful attack on an Israeli corvette by an anti-ship missile launched by Hezbollah elements near Beirut in 2006 is another.[11] Electronic attack in its modern cyber-warfare forms may well be adopted by insurgent groups, and even by criminal elements seeking to disrupt surveillance and enforcement efforts. All this means that medium navies need to consider comprehensive force protection as one of the foundations of their capability for operations in which *any* degree of armed conflict is possible, while civil agencies need not only to have their own protective measures, but be prepared to hand the task on. In this context, capability 'over-match' remains a good way of achieving necessary effects with the least casualties.

What do Medium Navies Need to Do?

Medium navies thus have many questions to answer in the second decade of the twenty-first century. On the other hand, these developments may not be as profound for the maritime environment as they are for the land. They may be changes which need to be dealt with imagination, rather than outright revolution. Naval forces by their nature possess a historical and cultural affinity for operations other than war to a far greater degree than is inherently true for armies and this remains true despite the recent experience of land operations in complex environments. It was international naval forces in the nineteenth century which played a critical part in the suppression of slave trading. Navies have been engaged in fishery protection and other constabulary tasks for hundreds of years, while the creation of ad hoc multinational maritime coalitions goes back nearly two centuries.[12]

This acceptance of roles additional to war-fighting has been recognised by many analysts and described most effectively by Booth, who explained that navies have three primary roles: war-fighting, constabulary and diplomatic.[13] One of his most important points was that the capacity which navies possess to accomplish the huge variety of diplomatic and constabulary tasks which they do from day to day rests largely upon the capabilities which they have developed for war-fighting. The 'triangle of operations' which has been developed to demonstrate this concept has been further modified.[14] A version developed in Australia shows the relationship between a nation's civil capability (in grey) and naval capability (in black) (Figure 1). This makes the point that operations under a legal mandate and those which are conducted under state authority in the interest of that state can have a wide range in the degree of force which may be required, but the greater the requirement the more that the responsibility passes to naval forces in their military roles.

Figure 1: The Span of Maritime Operations

Source: Author's Compilation

Achieving a Balanced Approach

The theme of complication extends to the methods and structures developed to meet national needs. Despite the obvious dangers in being prescriptive for a group of organisations of such complexity as medium navies, it is possible once the span of the operational requirement has been determined. to identify a number of key areas.

The goal of medium navies has always been to achieve the right balance of capabilities and the concept of the 'balanced fleet' must remain central to most of their planning for this era of complication. 'Balance', it must be emphasised, cannot be seen as an attempt to have something of everything. Rather, it should be the result of a judicious allocation of resources so as to provide governments with the greatest operational flexibility possible. Here, the concept of the triangle of maritime operations supports clarity of thought. Medium navies are defined fundamentally by their war-fighting capabilities and their primary effort needs to be directed towards an assessment of what is needed in this area, provided that all three elements remain borne firmly in mind.

Balance to Respond

Balance has two aspects that are important for medium navies. The first aspect is balance to protect against the unexpected threat. This concept is something that has a long history for navies, one that needs to be understood in an era when many observers are highlighting the existence of 'asymmetric threats' under the banner of the 'Revolution in Military Affairs' (RMA)—as if they were something new. They are not, and the very term 'balanced fleet' derives from the response necessary to the development of the first seagoing asymmetric threats in the modern era—the torpedo boat and the submarine—starting just over a century ago.[15] By integrating small craft, scouting vessels and capital ships and, later, aircraft, the maritime powers which sought to retain their ability to control the sea were able to reduce the threat to the extent to which they could achieve their ends.

The concept remains a central element of force planning for medium navies because, without a proper range of capabilities, they and their nations become immediately vulnerable to asymmetric threats in the maritime environment. Comprehensive force protection in a low-intensity conflict provides a good start to the possibilities which the medium navies need to encompass, because such force protection operations mirror those which can be described more broadly as 'maritime protective activities', such as the defence of merchant shipping and the protection of harbours, coasts, offshore installations and waterways from mines and from other attacks from the sea. This creates an obvious hierarchy of required activity. Mine countermeasures are essential to all medium navies. Maritime surveillance has already been discussed, but with these elements must also come an effective—and national, not just naval—maritime command, control and communications system.

The remainder of the range of capabilities within the order of battle of medium navies must depend upon their individual strategic requirements. If there is a need for the capacity to exercise sea denial, then a submarine force is likely to be a leading element. The surface combatant will also remain central to the operations for exercising sea control and supporting the projection of power. Anti-submarine warfare capabilities, albeit expensive, complex and difficult to maintain, must be a core element of the navy of any nation which is dependent upon the movement of shipping and has to achieve any degree of sea control.

Balance to Act

The second aspect of balance is the ability to do the unexpected, to provide options for national governments not only to react, but also to act. Medium navies must be about providing the maximum number of possibilities for their governments. Many of the force elements provide options, but in medium-power terms and in the context of an uncertain and dangerous world order, there are clear benefits in the possession of amphibious and logistics units and, just as important, of land forces which have the necessary equipment and expertise to operate in the maritime environment. It is also worth observing that some elements of the RMA, most notably unmanned vehicles and precision weapons, have the potential to give medium power surface combatants a utility in power projection against land which they have never enjoyed before.

It is unlikely that most medium powers will ever have the resources to conduct power projection operations in higher intensity conflicts unless in coalition. Nevertheless, being able to insert people, vehicles and logistic supplies without experiencing the need for developed facilities provides many possibilities for providing constructive responses to the unexpected. No nation is immune to natural disasters and seaborne means, particularly in Africa and the Asia-Pacific, may well be the *only* way through which a substantial relief effort can be mounted. Peace operations in a maritime region are likely to require significant maritime elements as well.

Joint Operations

There is another theme inherent in the concepts of balance—both in terms of threat and of action—for medium navies and that is the increasing requirement for effective joint operations with other national services. Medium powers cannot afford duplication between their individual services and the reality is that a credible national capability will depend increasingly upon the effective integration of all combat services. Very few medium navies can afford to sustain an organic combat in air and even when they do, their potential must be greatly increased by the careful coordination of carrier-borne aircraft with those based on land. No medium navy can sensibly contemplate sea control operations without the involvement of maritime patrol aircraft. Relatively, only a few medium navies can afford to maintain their own marine forces. Even if they can, the reality remains that these marines must develop close working relations with their armies. The list goes on.

Meeting the full range of national security requirements in areas such as surveillance and enforcement—particularly in the constabulary role—and the methods by which this is achieved are questions for the national decision-makers rather than for the navies alone. Whatever the approach taken, medium navies must be closely involved and the solution adopted must allow a coherent, systematic and comprehensive national effort. If the solution is to give the navy primacy in or a leading responsibility for civil surveillance and enforcement, then the force structure must allow for these activities without any detriment to its war-fighting capabilities. If there is a civil element, then it must not acquire capabilities which would be more useful to the governments than in naval hands.

On the other hand, even if the solution adopted is the formation of separate coast guards and even if these function wholly independent of any naval or military control, medium navies and maritime air forces will still have much to contribute in supplementing the surveillance effort and providing 'fall back' capabilities in the event of more complex or demanding operations, particularly those requiring the deployment of a substantial coercive force. The key requirement is for effective national command and control arrangements which ensure that there is no duplication of effort.

No matter what their individual situation, medium navies will need to sustain a very high degree of awareness of and expertise in surveillance and enforcement and take seriously their constabulary role. It follows in force structure terms that credible maritime surveillance capabilities are and will be inherent to an effective medium navy—as well as to a medium air force if it has the responsibility for maritime patrol aircraft—and that surveillance and response operations should be a significant element of naval and air force effort, whether in 'normal' conditions or in those of conflict.

Keeping Up with Technology

Still on the question of 'balance', medium navies have hard decisions to make about the extent to which they attempt to adopt the latest technology. It is easy to be caught in the situation of expending excessive funds and human resources in attempting to maintain elderly and obsolescent platforms and equipment. On the other hand, there may be no alternative if the capital costs of acquiring new technology are such that they cannot be afforded within the budget. In the case of medium and small navies, it is sometimes better to be able to do something badly than not to be able to do it at all.[16] The tests must always be: first, does the capability, however limited, present options which may prove vital to the national interest and which can be provided in no other way? Second, is the capability not being maintained at the expense of other more useful capabilities? It is possible to fall into the trap of pouring resources into one element of the fleet when others, equally vital to a medium power, are being neglected. If the capability passes these two tests—keep it.

People

Medium navies by their nature face many challenges in terms of structure and organisation. They place heavy demands on the domestic and hard currency resources of their governments. Navies require substantial industrial and technological infrastructure to support their activities—infrastructure which, in the case of smaller services, may seem disproportionate in relation to the combat capability which it generates.[17] Both in uniform and out of it, navies need the most highly educated and technically competent people that their countries have to offer, particularly in engineering and information systems. They are thus in direct competition for the resources on which nations are coming increasingly to depend for economic growth in an era of globalisation. Being instruments of the government, governed by its regulations and constraints, they are rarely in a position where they can offer a direct competition to business for the staff that they need. All too often, businesses leach from navies the people that the latter 'caught young' to train and educate. This is a syndrome that practically every modern navy has experienced in recent years, and which many are experiencing now. Conversely, however, navies suffer in periods of economic recession because of the inevitable reductions in national spending that follow—reductions to which navies are particularly vulnerable.[18]

Finding Solutions

Reducing the unfavourable ratio of support infrastructure to combat capability is where a division of 'back room' as well as 'up front' effort between partner navies can be so valuable. The question of autonomy, already raised, itself falls into three parts. The first is the extent to which a medium navy insists on operational autonomy by comparison with the degree to which it integrates with the operations of other navies. This will often be through the mechanism of formal alliances, but a degree of latent integration can also be achieved by cooperation outside the framework of alliances, a latency that governments may well find very valuable in an unexpected contingency when the national interest requires participation in an ad hoc coalition. What is clear is that achieving latent integration has a price, not in terms of political commitments, but in the degree to which resources—including steaming and training time—will need to be allocated to international cooperation rather than specific national tasking.

On the other hand, it is also true that cooperation greatly assists in establishing and maintaining benchmarks in terms of operational effectiveness and may well assist in achieving the necessary operational standards. Cooperation in the form of large multilateral exercises, for example, allows for economies of scale in the provision of targets and opposition forces which individual national forces cannot manage. The perils of conformity and group thinking can be avoided by exposure to different concepts, novel ideas and unfamiliar equipment. Navies do not prosper in isolation; like other complex organisations and professions, they need windows on the world to keep themselves up to date and effective.

The second aspect is the extent to which a nation concentrates on particular force elements in order to provide niche capabilities for cooperation with its partners. In some alliance circumstances, this may square the circle of restricted funding, in that it makes practical a contribution on a significant scale—big enough to be of more than a symbolic value. The risk with this approach is that it restricts the potential for individual national action and may create gaps in capability which create vulnerabilities in other contingencies.

The third is the extent of infrastructural (as opposed to operational) autonomy that a medium navy should seek. Only the United States Navy can seriously attempt to be on the cutting edge of every aspect of naval development and even this service is now under increasing pressure. Medium navies have to make clear choices between capabilities in which their requirements are such so as to produce unique systems and platforms and those which can be derived from the efforts of other countries. They have further choices to make in deciding how much they will do by themselves and how much they will cooperate with other navies or even rely upon others outright. Such a 'centre of excellence' approach is gathering strength in Western Europe and is likely to have much wider application. This is not only a question of alliances and political interests shared by nation-states permitting the necessary degree of cooperation; there are also highly complex problems relating to the involvement of domestic industry, technology transfer, intellectual property and, in particular, the provision of reliable and effective through-life support. Nevertheless it is clear that no medium power can afford to sustain all the costs of being a parent navy in every area of maritime warfare. Nor, if it wishes to spend its budget wisely, should it try. Arguably, this will become an increasingly critical problem for the 'human infrastructure' of many navies as the longer term effects of the progressive reductions in manpower which have been so commonly applied in recent years take effect and older, highly experienced staff retire without relief.

Conclusions

Medium navies must do much to survive. They need to develop and maintain a range of capabilities in order to provide the balance necessary to protect against threats in the maritime environment and to provide their governments with the widest possible range of options. Medium navies need to make hard decisions regarding the extent to which they will be autonomous in comparison to the degree to which they will cooperate with other nations and navies in acquiring and maintaining their capabilities.

Medium navies need to work closely with their national air forces and armies and with civil security agencies to achieve the most effective results for national security. Above all, medium navies need to understand themselves and their situations, and be much better than many have been in the past at explaining their roles to themselves and to others. Indeed, perhaps the greatest challenge they face is that of justifying their place in a constantly changing world to people and authorities who have little affinity with, and a lesser understanding of, the maritime domain.

Author's Note

This paper is the product of research undertaken over the last twelve months, and which is still continuing. It develops the author's own ideas set out in "The Role of the Medium Power Navy in the Twenty-First Century" Jurgen Schwarz, Wilfried A. Herrmann & Hanns-Frank Seller (eds), *Maritime Strategies in Asia,* White Lotus, Bangkok, 2002, pp. 57-71. I am very grateful to the Warden and Fellows of All Souls College at the University of Oxford for the opportunity to undertake a visiting fellowship on this project in the first half of 2015.

Notes

1. Hill, J. R. *Maritime Strategy for Medium Powers*. London: Croom Helm, 1986, p.21. See also, Hill, Richard *Medium Power Strategy Revisited,* RAN Sea Power Centre, Working Paper No. 3, March 2000, pp.4-5.
2. Richard Hill *Medium Power Strategy Revisited,* Note 1, p.7.
3. For an Australian perspective, see RAN Doctrine 1: *Australian Maritime Doctrine,* (Second edition) Canberra, 2010. p. 68.
4. The development in the direction of expeditionary operations was particularly evident when the text of the 1999 edition of *British Maritime Doctrine* is compared with the previous (1995) edition of *BR 1806: The Fundamentals of British Maritime Doctrine.* This has continued with more recent editions, including the current *British Maritime Doctrine* (Joint Doctrine Publication 0-10 of 2011). For the beginning of the United States' impetus see *From the Sea: Preparing the Naval Service for the 21st Century* United States Navy, Washington DC, 1992. More recent US efforts, notably *A Cooperative Strategy for 21st Century Seapower* have a much stronger maritime security element. http://www.navy.mil/local/maritime/150227-CS21R-Final.pdf.
5. Gray, Colin S. *Modern Strategy*. New York: Oxford University Press, 1999, pp. 218-219.
6. For statistics and analysis see the International Maritime Organization website: http://www.imo.org/OurWork/Security/PiracyArmedRobbery/Pages/Default.aspx .
7. In the five months up to February 2016, the Australian frigate HMAS *Melbourne* on CMF operations as part of Task Force 150 in the Indian Ocean and Arabian Sea intercepted some 977 kg of illegal drugs with a street value of $AUS 390 million. http://navaltoday.com/2016/02/11/hmas-melbourne-concludes-middle-eastern-deployment/?uid=529.
8. One of the best start-of-the-century assessments—not wholly focused on the American situation—was found in Stubbs, Bruce B., Scott C. Truver, and Edward Feege. *America's Coast Guard: Safeguarding U.S. Maritime Safety and Security in the 21st*

Century. Washington, D.C.: Assistance Commandant, Operations (G-O), U.S. Coast Guard Headquarters, 2000, especially Chapter II. The great majority of the analysis remains valid, despite the passage of 15 years and it has had a clear influence on *A Cooperative Strategy for 21st Century Seapower*.

9. Parry, Chris. *Super Highway: Sea Power in the 21st Century*. London: Elliott and Thompson, 2014, p. 340.
10. See, Friedman, Norman. *Seapower and Space: From the Dawn of the Missile Age to Net-centric Warfare*. Annapolis, MD: Naval Institute Press, 2000.
11. Although the Israelis allege that the Hezbollah elements had the support of trained Iranian Revolutionary Guard (Navy) personnel. http://news.bbc.co.uk/1/hi/world/middle_east/5242566.stm.
12. Arguably starting with the Anglo-Dutch bombardment of Algiers in 1816 over the slavery issue. While such activities were often for imperialist or mercantilist purposes (the intervention in China in 1900 and the blockade of Venezuela in 1903), there were also interventions for disaster relief. The multinational effort after the 1908 earthquake in the Sicilian city of Messina is one example. For a chronology of the Royal Navy's activities in the nineteenth and early twentieth century, see *The Royal Navy List or Who's Who in the Navy London,* January 1917.Republished as *The Naval Who's Who 1917* J.B. Hayward, Suffolk, 1981, pp. 211-217.
13. Booth, Ken. *Navies and Foreign Policy*. London: Croom Helm, 1977, p.16.
14. See Grove, Eric. *The Future of Sea Power*. Annapolis, Md: Naval Institute Press, 1990, pp. 232-235.
15. See in particular, Sumida, Jon Tetsuro. *In Defence of Naval Supremacy: Finance, Technology, and British Naval Policy, 1889-1914*. Boston: Unwin Hyman, 1989, and; Lambert, Nicholas A. *Sir John Fisher's Naval Revolution*. Columbia, S.C.: University of South Carolina Press, 1999.
16. See this argument developed in the author's *No Easy Answers: The Development of the Navies of India, Pakistan, Bangladesh, and Sri Lanka, 1945-1996. New Delhi: Lancer Publishers, 1997* pp. 201-202, as well as Goldrick, James, and Jack McCaffrie. *Navies of South-East Asia: A Comparative Study*. Milton Park, Abingdon, Oxon: Routledge, 2013.
17. For an assessment of the issues involved in analysing naval activity see Jon Tetsuro Sumida and David Rosenberg 'Machines, Men, Manufacturing, Management and Money: the Study of Navies as Complex Organisations and the Transformation of Twentieth Century Naval History' in John B. Hattendorf, John B. *Doing Naval History: Essays Toward Improvement*. Newport, R.I.: Naval War College Press, 1995, pp. 25-40.
18. For a perspective on the issues of navies in developing nations in particular see the author's *No Easy Answers*, Note 16, Chapter 9.

6. Maritime Cooperation and Building Bridges between Maritime Neighbours and Partners

Renfrew Christie

Introduction

The Indo-Pacific region is the centre of the future of humanity. China's economy has risen profoundly and it is hoped that India's will do the same. Africa's population will more than double by 2050, giving a vast economic opportunity. Growth will demand both peace and expanded free trade at sea, especially in the Indo-Pacific region. To achieve peace, trade and growth, bigger and better navies are needed in the Indo-Pacific, and they must cooperate. Without peace, enforced by strong, collaborating navies, so that the vast economic advantages of sea trade may be harvested, the future of the Indo-Pacific region will in all likelihood be Hobbesian. During war, Hobbes wrote, there are

> "No arts; no letters; no society; and which is worst of all, continual fear, and danger of violent death: and the life of man, solitary, poor, nasty, brutish and short".[1]

The opposite of war and want are the sumptuous economic benefits of peace; benefits only made possible by a global free trade at sea and secured by strong navies, as exemplified by the Chinese triumph.

China could only rise because the United States Navy was protecting the world's seaborne trade, but the US will no longer do that to the same extent. Japan, with a long-term economic deflation and a matching and rapidly ageing population,[2] is bravely attempting a naval expansion.[3] However, with so old a population, Japan must inevitably play a diminishing naval role in the longer term. Europe too is ageing and its naval power waning. It will be argued that the navies of Africa, India and China must fill the gap.

The United States Navy has enabled the Rise of China by Securing World Shipping

In 1945, China's population was large; its economy was small; its GDP per capita reflected appalling misery; and its seaborne trade was tiny. By 2015, China had changed and had taken its rightful place in the world. China's population, its GDP and its sea trade are now nearly twenty per cent of the world's figures; but, China rose under US naval protection.[4]

In 2015, Martin Stopford analysed the American philosophy, with its free-trade enablement of shipping, which had allowed China to rise:

> "By the 1960s, a century of serving the European empires was ending and shipping's new role was globalisation. This came as a result of nations in Asia and Africa being granted independence and the establishment of the European Union in 1958. The US, the world's wealthiest economy, provided a political hegemony founded on the principles of free trade, established at the Bretton Woods conference in 1944, and the rapidly expanding multi-national companies managed the change. The result was spectacular trade growth. Sea trade expanded from 1.6bn tonnes in 1965 to 10.3bn tonnes in 2015, a six-fold increase."[5]

In 2012, Martin Stopford recorded that while the world economy had grown by eight times since 1950, the sea trade had grown sixteen times, or in other words, twice as fast.[6] Increased safe shipping underpinned the global economic growth and most of the expansion took place after the end of the Cold War, with China in the lead.

China took advantage of the Naval *Pax Americana,* to achieve its 'instant noodles' miracle. China used its vast seaborne trade to grow its economy, at a speed and to a size to which only a few had ever dreamed. China's seaborne imports in the first fifteen years of the twenty-first century grew by nine times, or by two thousand million tonnes; from 240 million tonnes in the year 2000 to 2,240 million tonnes in 2014.[7] Chinese container trade alone grew from 41 million TEU in 2000 to 174 million TEU in 2013, while in the same period USA's container trade only moved from 28 million TEU to 44 million TEU.[8] Clarkson's Research sums it up:

> "China has long been at the heart of the expansion in global seaborne trade. Between 2002 and 2014, four billion tons were added to the world seaborne total. Chinese imports accounted for 94% of the increase in iron ore volumes, 35% of the expansion in coal volumes and equivalent to more than 100% of the growth in crude oil trade. Chinese exports accounted for around 60% of the expansion in container trade volumes."[9]

China's achievement was unique in history. Hundreds of millions of people moved quickly from the rice paddies into the cities and joined the middle class. In 1990, 61% of the Chinese people were extremely poor but by 2015 only 4% of the Chinese people were in extreme poverty.[10] China produced seven per cent of the world's steel in 1989[11], but by 2014 it was suddenly producing half the steel on earth.[12] China was set to be the richest country in the world; but, its 'instant noodle' wealth revolution was impossible without a safe sea trade.

Who will secure the Indo-Pacific Trade as the US Navy declines?

Which navies will secure the continuing rise of China; then that of India and then that of Africa?

The German armed forces, including the navy, are in decline.[13] France is cutting its numbers of sailors and ships.[14] In 1919, the British Royal Navy had four aircraft carriers and three thousand fixed-wing aircraft.[15] Today it has no carriers and no fixed-wing aircraft. By 2025 it may have carriers again; but how many Lightning F35B fixed wing aircraft will be aboard them is unknown.[16]

The United States Navy is cutting back. *CNN*'s Zachary Cohen reported: "The U.S. naval force is currently made up of 273 ships, which is the smallest number since the fleet stood at 245 ships in 1916".[17] The US Navy's decline is written into its strategy. There is a reverted Kiplingesque[18] desire that others must take up Teddy Roosevelt's Great White Fleet's burden. Reviewing the March 2015 version of the US Naval Strategy, Geoffrey Till has noted a diminished American willingness to defend the world's seaways. Till emphasises that among the all the problems is one of financial cost.

> "This reduced emphasis on the systemic justification for U.S. sea power doubtless reflects the fact that in the 2007 version of the strategy, it did not go down well in Congress—which ultimately pays the Navy's bills."[19]

The American people are increasingly unwilling either to pay for or to drown for economic growth in other peoples' countries. The proof of the US Navy's decline is that ships at sea, on both sides of Africa and throughout the Indian Ocean, identify themselves on tracking sites as having 'Armed Guards Aboard'.[20] Quite when the US Navy will cease to police all the oceans is not clear, but, sooner or later, Africa, China and India must collaboratively secure their own economic triumphs, using their own navies. India seeks to follow China's economic triumph. By the time China ages, a larger Indian workforce must also urbanise and enter the middle class. Thereafter, the African giant must rise in the same way. We will see that by 2050, between half and two-thirds of all humans will live in Africa, China and India. If they are to be fed, healthy, housed and happy, Africa must be at peace, while China and India must not go to war. Moreover, sea trade must be protected so that the economies can thrive. Neither the United States nor Western Europe will sufficiently police the Indo-Pacific Region's oceans in the longer run. Peaceful maritime self-security is the lynchpin for prosperity in Africa, China and India. The Indo-Pacific Region must defend its own oceans, spending its own treasure on warships and risking its own sailors. A retired Indian Navy admiral has phrased the need in another way:

> "The challenge for Mr Modi is to avoid getting India sucked into the conflict [with China and Pakistan], while expanding the role and reach of the Navy. India needs to enhance its defence and homeland security capabilities (and raise military morale) while creating the climate to ensure that India's economic growth of 7.5 percent not only continues but also crosses 8 percent so that our present $2 trillion GDP reaches $5 trillion by 2025. Hopefully it will reach $25 trillion in 2050, by which time India should be a superpower with a three-ocean Navy capable of serving our national interests in the Pacific, Atlantic and Indian Oceans."[21]

Becoming a superpower in thirty-five years is rare in history, because it requires almost impossible economic growth rates. Admiral Singh's ambition, quoted above, is praiseworthy in wanting India to grow at over 8% per annum; but, as the following study from the St Louis Fed demonstrates, an 11% growth rate would be better:

> "It is even harder to imagine that such [developing] countries could reach U.S. living standards within one to two generations (40 to 50 years), similar to how North American and Western European economies caught up to Britain during the 1800s after the Industrial Revolution. To achieve that speed of convergence today, the developing countries would need to grow about 8 percentage points faster than the U.S. (or about 11 percent per year) nonstop for 40 to 50 years. In recent history, only China came close to this; it was able to maintain a 10 percent annual growth rate (7 percentage points above the U.S. rate) for 35 years, but per capita income in China was still only one-seventh of that in the U.S. in 2014."[22]

The coming 35 years will of course see economic crashes as well as booms. An 11 per cent annual GDP growth rate, on an average, may well prove to be impossible. Using less ambitious assumptions, the Price Waterhouse Coopers model expects India to have the same GDP as America in 2050,[23] which means that its s GDP per capita will still be substantially less than the US's. Even so, the Indian Ocean sea routes will need protection if India is to blossom.

Reducing the Indo-Pakistani Conflict

Whether India will achieve very high growth rates is unknown; however, what is clear is that high growth rates demand peace and freedom of seaborne trade. India and Pakistan may find that they both need more sea trade to expand their economies. If so, their joint protection of the routes through the Indian Ocean may be seen to be in both their interests than fanning the fading historical flames of conflict between them.

On Christmas Day 2015, Prime Minister Narendra Modi made a surprise stop to visit his counterpart Nawaz Sharif in Lahore. After the meeting, Pakistan's Foreign Secretary, Aizaz Chaudhry, said "Among the decisions taken was that ties between the two countries would be strengthened and also people-to-people contact would be strengthened so that the atmosphere can be created in which the peace process can move forward."[24]

Earlier, in Kabul, PM Modi had urged that there be peace in the region and especially between Pakistan and India. "We know that Afghanistan's success will require the cooperation and support of each of its neighbours," he said. "And all of us in the region – India, Pakistan, Iran and others – must unite in trust and cooperation behind the common purpose and in recognition of our common destiny."[25]

'Common destiny' implies common interests. If India and Pakistan are to see their economies boom in the way China's has, they will need the peace and security of seaborne trade. If and when the United States Navy reduces its commitments, the navies of India and Pakistan must cooperate peacefully. This will also require an Indian rapprochement with China.

Fast Population Expansion Requires Greater Sea Trade Protected by Bigger Navies

Humans will *quadruple* their numbers between 1950 and 2050. Using our best demographic model,[26] we found that there were 2,510 million people in 1950. Humans *tripled* in sixty-five years, to 7,349 million people alive today. The expansion rate will decrease, resulting in 9,725 million living in 2050. China's population grew from 543 million in 1950 to 1,376 million today, and will drop slightly to 1,348 million in 2050.

India had 375 million people in 1950; and has 1,311 million today. It will have 1,705 million people in 2050. That is, India will be bigger than China by 357 million people in 2050. Therefore, the *difference* between India and China in 2050 will approximate the *entire* Indian population of 375 million in 1950.

Africa had 228 million people in 1950; but it is over *four times* larger today at 1,186 million; and, will more than *double again* to 2,478 million in 2050. So, the population of Africa in 2050 will almost equal that of the whole world in 1950.

By 2050, the most spectacular population growth will be seen in Africa. Nigeria will be bigger than the USA. In round numbers, China will be two and-a-half times larger in 2050 than in 1950; the world will be four times larger; India will be four-and-a-half times larger: while Africa will be *eleven* times larger than it was in 1950.

These huge population levels will change world politics, economics and trade. Today's powerful, rich countries will be older, smaller, poorer states by 2050. The growth areas—Africa, India and China— must prepare now for their new responsibilities. Their seaborne trade must grow significantly if there is to be prosperity. To protect the shipping, they must build new navies.

Shipping and World Trade have Hugely Increased but Northern Navies have been Cut

Shipping has grown alongside the world economy and more, bigger and better commercial ships are now being used. The tonnage of commercial ships in 1910 was 41 million tonnes compared to 958 million tonnes in 2010. In 2010, there were three times more commercial ships, and they were almost seven times bigger.[27] The new large ships, which are the basis of world trade, grew from 14,000 vessels in 1965 to just under 50,000 in 2014.[28] The biggest ships today are 6,00,000 tonnes and half-a-kilometre long.[29] World shipping today is enormous.

However, navies have not kept pace. For example, Ben Wilson records that the British Royal Navy had 760 ships in 1918 but 76 ships in 2012. In 1918, it had 4,37,000 sailors, reduced to 30,000 by 2010.[30] Let us look at the shrinking of the US Navy. It is also cancelling orders of the Zumwalt destroyers[31] and Littoral Combat Ships.[32] Germany no longer pretends and the query posed in 2006 was "Where is the German CVN aircraft-carrier?"[33] The North Atlantic powers have cut their navies and will reduce further; also, they will reduce their investment for the protection of the Indo-Pacific Region.

Clearly, the world population sizes and trading patterns are changing rapidly. If India and Africa wish to emulate China's prosperity, they must have China's high levels of sea trade. China must maintain those levels, or slide economically. The North Atlantic interest is shrinking. Imports to the OECD countries, 'the home of traditional seafarers', have shrunk from two-thirds of world trade in 1965 to one-third now.[34] The North Atlantic powers will stop defending the non-OECD sea trade. Africa, India and China must build bigger, better navies to protect the sea trade in order to grow their economies. And they must avoid war, which destroys proper economic growth.

Air Forces, Missiles, Drones and New Technologies cannot Substitute for Ships at Sea

It may be argued that advanced air forces, space warfare, rocketry, drones and the new technologies coming from advanced research institutions like the US's Defense Advanced Research Projects Agency (DARPA),[35] may have rendered navies outmoded and redundant. With modern electronic target acquisition, high-speed planes and missiles, satellite surveillance, undersea listening devices and reduced circular error probabilities which are approaching pinpoint accuracy; it may be found that surface ships and submarine boats will all be sunk very quickly in a real war. DARPA is conducting research whose results are likely to strengthen an attack from the air:

> "Maintaining air superiority in contested environments; leading the world in advanced hypersonics; (precise warhead delivery at hypersonic velocities is a significant opportunity to change the pace of warfare)".[36]

On the other hand, DARPA is also "enhancing maritime agility". It explains:

> "Oceans are strategically central but almost incomprehensibly large, demanding innovative approaches to achieve strategic leverage."[37]

Therefore, DARPA itself identifies the problem with the idea that navies have been outmoded by technology: Oceans are strategically central but almost incomprehensibly large. Only ships and submarines can deal with the size of the oceans. Just as on land there is no substitute for humans in 'boots on the ground', at sea, the crucial mode of warfare must remain surface and undersea vessels, with highly trained sailors to man them. This is the 'boats in the water' rule, matching the 'boots on the ground' rule.

There are judgement calls at sea, which only humans can make; in the same way, knowing whether a prospective target is a wedding party or a terrorist cell is easier on the ground than at ten thousand metres up. No drone strike or hypersonic missile can deal with pirates aboard an oil tanker, who have taken the crew hostage.

By 2050, the technological change may be expected to be as profound and radical as that of the last thirty-five years; which weapons will work in the future we do not know, but the endless rivalry between defence and attack will not go away. Ships will be sunk by new technology and ships will defeat new methods of assault; but, navies are here to stay.

The US 'Pivot' is to the Pacific; but the Oil Choke Points are in the Indian Ocean

What is the intent of the 'Rebalance' of the United States towards the Far East? "Asia and the Pacific is increasingly the world's political and economic centre of gravity"; therefore "The U.S. [has a] Vision for Asia and the Pacific"; and so the Presidential Fact Sheet is entitled *Advancing the Rebalance to Asia and the Pacific.*[38] Africa, India and the Indian Ocean are afterthoughts, or add-ons, to the thrust at the Asian Pacific. The White House's words forget Africa completely, whereas the hope is that India will defend itself:

> "Expanding and deepening U.S. engagement with India in the Asia Pacific and Indian Ocean region is an important element of the Rebalance. We welcome India's positive role in ensuring a stable, peaceful, and prosperous region."[39]

However, Indian Navy Captain Raghavendra Mishra has argued that *for India* the *Indian Ocean* is central:

> "The primacy of the Indian Ocean in the [Indian] national strategic calculus is far more critical due to energy dependency on the Middle East, increasing economic linkages with Africa, and the security of major sea lines of communication passing through the western Indian Ocean."[40]

The Indian Ocean matters to the whole world more than any other. It is the most important energy trade route on earth, shipping fossil fuels not merely to the US and the erstwhile European allies, but also to the focus of the 'Rebalance', that is, to China, Japan and Korea. Russian energy exports to China are increasing, but China's other big sources are Angola, Oman and Saudi Arabia—all three of which use the Indian Ocean to get their product to China.[41]

The US Energy Information Agency (EIA) lists seven maritime choke points: the Straits of Hormuz and of Malacca, the Suez Canal with the

SUMED Pipeline, the Bab el-Mandeb (or Gate of Tears), the Danish Straits, the Turkish Straits and the Panama Canal. The last three are not on the Indian Ocean, and are negligible. In 2013, the four Indian Ocean choke points carried almost ninety per cent of the world maritime traded oil and petroleum products. Put another way, the four Indian Ocean choke points carried over half of the world's total oil supply in 2013.[42]

The EIA addresses the Cape of Good Hope, but does not term it as a choke point.

> "Although not a chokepoint, the Cape of Good Hope is a major global trade route. Crude oil flows around the Cape accounted for about 9% of all seaborne-traded oil."[43]

The EIA assessment is misplaced. Originally known as the Cape of Storms, it is a choke point. It is possible to sail Very Large Crude Carriers (VLCC) through the 'roaring forties', but not desirable. It is an exercise in threading a needle and making the ships vulnerable. During the Second World War, the Japanese and Nazi submarines sank close to 150 ships in the South African waters. Closing the Cape today would be simple. The *2015 Indian Maritime Security Strategy* recognises a South West Indian Ocean choke point, beginning in the Mozambique Channel.[44]

The United States' 'pivot' is clearly to the Asia-Pacific and neglects the Indian Ocean. At present, the United States, Western Europe and other navies have an interest to keep the Indian Ocean open. In an age of proxy wars, Somali piracy became an excellent source of pretence, enabling ships from thirty navies to cluster conveniently near Hormuz, Suez and Bab el-Mandeb. But in 2050, when Nigeria is bigger than the US, and when Africa, India and China put together are twelve times bigger than the US as well, it must be their own navies which should be protecting the choke points.

The Navies and Maritime Air Forces of the Indo-Pacific Region are Unequal to the Task

The navies of the Indo-Pacific are unequal to the task of ensuring free trade at sea. They have too few new platforms, too few sailors and pilots, too few highly skilled leaders and exercise together too seldom—all of which affects their ability to win just wars, keep proper peace, maintain the safety of the vast oceans, or even to survive the first month of an all-out twenty-first-century-non-nuclear warfare.

Peacetime navies are not designed for wartime attrition. It may be recalled that in 1904–5, Japan destroyed two-thirds of the Russian fleet. In 1914, Britain lost sixteen warships.[45] In 1939–1940, Britain lost 71 vessels. Almost half of the 1939 Royal Navy had been sunk by 1945.[46] The Kriegsmarine lost 47 ships and 780 submarines in WWII, while Japan lost 209 warships and 127 submarines.[47] The attrition at Pearl Harbour is legendary. In six weeks of 1982, 23 British ships were hit; six were sunk and three more badly damaged, while another thirteen would have been sunk had the bomb fuses been correctly set.[48]

To the problem of attrition must be added that of availability. Navies struggle to train and retain skilled sailors, without whom no ship goes to sea. But even with perfectly available crews, a ship must have major and minor repairs. A lack of crews, fuel or parts results in excessive ship downtime.

German technology is excellent; yet of Germany's twenty frigates, corvettes and submarines, only ten were said to be deployable in 2014.[49] South Africa has four frigates and three submarines; at good times, three of the frigates and two of the submarines are seen at sea; yet sometimes, there is one of each. If the Cape of Storms has to be defended during one bad winter, with nine per cent of the world's seaborne oil flows at stake, one frigate and one submarine cannot do the defensive job. The attack is easier: one submarine, skilfully handled, can close the Straits of Malacca.

The US Navy has astounding logistics; yet for US home-ported ships, the number of days 'deployed under way', in 2012, was a mean of 70 days out of 366. For ships exceptionally home-ported overseas, the figure was 118. The US Navy ships are available for one-sixth of the year.[50]

To be generous, assume that a ship is available for one-third of a year. The following navies have the following totals of destroyers, frigates and corvettes,[51] therefore the number of available ships can be calculated: China 95 (36); India 49 (16); Indonesia 26 (9); Egypt 15 (5); Australia 12 (4); Pakistan 10 (3); South Africa 4 (1); Nigeria 2 (1); while Kenya has only coastal defence craft totalling 7 (2). In emergency; or for exercises, greater numbers of ships can be available.

These navies must replace the North Atlantic forces. Provided they are not at war with each other, and noting that the Chinese Navy has greater Pacific responsibilities, the possible total of available is 41 vessels (or 59 if half of the available Chinese ships are allocated to the Indian Ocean). These vessels would have to protect the flow of ninety per cent of the world's seaborne oil. The distances to be traversed are from Lagos to the Straits of Malacca. Moreover, recall the certainty of attrition in twenty-first century naval warfare: 35 of the 41 non-Chinese ships could well be sunk in the first week of conflict.

In sum, it is difficult to defend the Indian Ocean. There is lack of experience in joint operations, in ensuring proper naval and air firepower, working with land forces and in keeping the peace in the vital

100-kilometre littoral. Similarly, the budgets and the vision are too small. The political, economic and military leadership needs a rejigging to the great task at hand.

National Consensuses on Navies, Naval Bases, Logistics and Continuous Shipbuilding

The transition from the North Atlantic navies, to those of Africa, India and China, in the Indian Ocean Region (IOR) is vital to the future of humanity, because Africa, India and China will contain some three-fifths of all humans by 2050. Their politico-economic future depends on fast growing economies supplied by the world sea trade. Bigger, better navies must be built; starting now.

Historically, hegemony over the oceans has enabled prodigious economic growth, based on the divisions of labour, comparative advantages and the benefits of scale, which safe seaborne trade optimises. Simply, Britain fought for some hundreds of years, before the Royal Navy could rule the world's oceans from 1815 to 1914. The two world wars and the great depression were an interregnum. Since 1945, the United States Navy has ruled. At some time the US will yield hegemony to one or more of the other navies—probably drawn from Africa, India and China.

N.A.M Rodger concludes in his majestic analysis[52] of how Britain came to rule the waves that the goal was not empire or world domination, but defence from invasion. The key was national consensus; keeping a winning navy was vital and existential. Provided all agreed about the centrality of the Royal Navy to the protection of all that was British, victory was possible.

> "[A] strong, consistent and broad-based political support for a costly Navy distinguishes Britain from all other European powers...Only the unwavering support of the political nation, sustained over decades, if not centuries, could build up a dominant sea power."[53]

Yet this was not enough. Until 1815, the Royal Navy was Britain's biggest industry. It stimulated the economy with its naval bases and dockyards; its intertwined and complicated logistics involved agriculture and manufacturing, science and invention and continuous building and maintenance of its ships and their crews. "The Navy protected the trade and protected the country. Trade generated the seamen to man the navy and the money to pay for it".[54] A national consensus led via a continuous national industry to a national victory at sea.

"Only when ships could be kept at sea with healthy crews for long periods could the possibilities of naval power be fully exploited. Thus the final achievement of naval supremacy, after so many false starts and disappointments, was a truly national achievement which drew on the economic and social resources of the three kingdoms to sustain professional sea power at war."[55]

The same may apply to the states of Africa, India, and China, who come to replace the United States Navy in the Indian Ocean. They will need a national consensus: that the expensive, lengthy task of making and maintaining a winning Navy is vital to all their interests. They will need endless shore-based industry, supplies, dockyards, naval bases and logistics. And, they will need an unremitting, continuous building of ships[56] and crews, without which there will be no freedom of seaborne trade and, hence, no economic growth. They may also have to reconcile themselves to a collaborative naval hegemony for the sake of peace and prosperity.

Conclusion

The alternative outcome to the propositions here is that India and China will not build navies to replace that of the United States in protecting trade in the Indo-Pacific, and especially in the crucial Indian Ocean. Africa, too, will not build navies proportional to its trade need and expected enormous population. Instead of opening complete free trade with each other (which would build the greatest single market in human history), India and China will go to war with each other. China will use Pakistan as a pawn in the process. Attrition in the small navies will be so destructive that seaborne trade will cease for the lack of protection. The world economy will stagger and fall. Hobbes will win his war.

Author's Note

This chapter takes forward ideas discussed in Renfrew Christie, "The Implications of Demographic and Economic Change for the African Maritime Arena", *Journal of the Indian Ocean Region,* Volume 12, Issue 1, 2016, Special Issue, The Indian Ocean Dialogue: An Evolving forum for Indian Ocean Maritime Security Issues, pp. 67-74, using an updated, more recent version of the UN world population statistics. Anyone writing on the field of commercial shipping must fully acknowledge the extensive data and argument put publicly on the web by Clarkson's Research and Martin Stopford; I do so with gratitude.

Notes

1. Hobbes, Thomas. *Leviathan*, 1651, Chapter 12.
2. Canon, Maria E., Kudlyak, Maryanna and Reid. Marisa. "Aging and the Economy: The Japanese Experience", *The St Louis Fed*, October 2015 https://www.stlouisfed.org/publications/regional-economist/october-2015/aging-and-the-economy-the-japanese-experience?utm_source=Research&utm_medium=Newsletter&utm_campaign=201511B.
3. McCurry, Justin. "Japan Signs Off Biggest Ever Defence Budget as Senkaku Tensions Rise", *The Guardian*, 24 December 2015, http://www.theguardian.com/world/2015/dec/24/japan-approves-defence-budget-china-senkaku.
4. Stopford, Martin. "China at a Turning Point: From the Trade Development Cycle to the One Belt One Road Concept", 8 September 2015, Fig. 6, https://www.city.ac.uk/__data/assets/pdf_file/0010/289189/CF-Stopford,-M.pdf.
5. Stopford, Martin. "Will the Next 50 years be as Chaotic as the Last?", 15 May 2015, http://www.lloydslist.com/ll/sector/ship-operations/article461048.ece?service=print.
6. Stopford, Martin. "Can Shipping Meet the Challenge of Change?", Second Annual INMAREST Lecture, 20 November 2012, https://www.youtube.com/watch?v=QAOMio-w2vQ.
7. Clarkson's Research, "What's Left in Shipping's Aladdin's Cave, Captain?", 17 October 2014, https://clarksonsresearch.wordpress.com/2014/10/17/whats-left-in-shippings-aladdins-cave-captain/.
8. World Bank, Container port traffic (TEU: 20 foot equivalent units) | Data | Table, http://data.worldbank.org/indicator/IS.SHP.GOOD.TU.
9. Clarkson's Research, "All Change or Play It Again: Which Scenario to Pick?", 26 June 2016, https://clarksonsresearch.wordpress.com/2015/06/26/all-change-or-play-it-again-which-scenario-to-pick/.
10. United Nations, *The Millennium Development Goals Report 2015*, (United Nations, New York, July 2015), p. 14.
11. International Iron and Steel Institute, *Steel Statistical Yearbook 1999*, Table B1, https://www.worldsteel.org/dms/internetDocumentList/statistics-archive/yearbook-archive/Steel-statisitical-yearbook-1999/document/Steel%20statistical%20yearbook%201999.pdf.
12. World Steel Association, *Steel Statistical Yearbook 2015*, Table One, https://www.worldsteel.org/dms/internetDocumentList/bookshop/2015/Steel-Statistical-Yearbook-2015/document/Steel%20Statistical%20Yearbook%202015.pdf.
13. *Der Spiegel* Staff, "Germany's Disarmed Forces: Ramshackle Military at Odds with Global Aspirations", *Der Spiegel*, 30 September 2014, http://www.spiegel.de/international/germany/ramshackle-army-at-odds-with-berlin-s-global-aspirations-a-994607.html.
14. Tran, Pierre. "French Navy Plans To Dominate Above, On and Below the Seas", *Defense News*, 26 October 2014, http://archive.defensenews.com/article/20141026/DEFREG01/310260022/French-Navy-Plans-Dominate-Above-Below-Seas ; and France, Ministry of Defence, *White Paper on Defence and National Security*, July 2013,

p.91 http://www.defense.gouv.fr/english/content/download/206186/2393586/file/White%20paper%20on%20defense%20%202013.pdf.

15. Ben, Wilson. *Empire of the Deep: the Rise and Fall of the British Navy*, London, Weidenfield and Nicholson, 2014, p. 554.
16. Freedberg, Sydney J. "UK Commits To 2 Carriers, Fully Crewed; F-35B Numbers To Be Determined", *Breaking Defense*, 4 September 2015, http://breakingdefense.com/2015/09/uk-commits-to-2-carriers-fully-crewed-f-35b-numbers-tbd/.
17. Cohen, Zachary. "Size Matters: Is the U.S. Navy Really Too Small?" *CNN Politics* http://edition.cnn.com/2015/09/08/politics/us-navy-size-military-election-2016/
18. Kipling, Rudyard. "The White Man's Burden: The United States & the Philippine Islands, 1899", *Rudyard Kipling's Verse: Definitive Edition*, New York, Doubleday, 1929.
19. Till, Geoffrey. "The New US Maritime Strategy: Another View From The Outside", *Naval War College Review*, Autumn 2015 Volume 68, Number 4 pp.35 -36, http://www.hsdl.org/?view&did=787201.
20. Marine Traffic, *Ships Map: Vessel Tracking & AIS Positions Map*, http://www.marinetraffic.com/en/ais/home.
21. Singh, A. S., "The Indian Navy's blue-water quest", *Asian Age*, 3 December 2015, http://www.asianage.com/columnists/indian-navy-s-blue-water-quest-738.
22. Arias, Maria A. and Yi Wen, "Trapped: Few Developing Countries Can Climb the Economic Ladder or Stay There", The St Louis Fed, *The Regional Economist*, October 2015, p.5, https://www.stlouisfed.org/publications/regional-economist/october-2015/trapped-few-developing-countries-can-climb-the-economic-ladder-or-stay-there.
23. PricewaterhouseCoopers, *The World in 2050: Will the Shift in Global Economic Power Continue?*, February 2015, Figure 6, page 10, http://www.pwc.com/gx/en/issues/the-economy/assets/world-in-2050-february-2015.pdf.
24. Reuters' New Delhi, "Indian Prime Minister makes Surprise Stopover in Pakistan", *The Guardian*, 25 December 2015, http://www.theguardian.com/world/2015/dec/25/indian-prime-minister-makes-surprise-stopover-in-pakistan.
25. Reuters' New Delhi, "Indian Prime Minister makes Surprise Stopover in Pakistan", *The Guardian*, 25 December 2015, http://www.theguardian.com/world/2015/dec/25/indian-prime-minister-makes-surprise-stopover-in-pakistan; see also Ellen Barry and Salman Masooddec, "Narendra Modi of India Meets Pakistani Premier in Surprise Visit", *New York Times*, 25 December 2015, http://www.nytimes.com/2015/12/26/world/asia/narendra-modi-nawaz-sharif-india-pakistan.html?emc=edit_th_20151226&nl=todaysheadlines&nlid=32507561&_r=0.
26. United Nations, Department of Economic and Social Affairs, Population Division, *World Population Prospects: The 2015 Revision, Key Findings and Advance Tables*, United Nations, New York, 2015, http://esa.un.org/unpd/wpp/Publications/Files/Key_Findings_WPP_2015.pdf, Medium Variant, as recorded for ease of access in Martin de Wulf, *Population Pyramids of the World from 1950 to 2100*, http://populationpyramid.net/world/2050/.
27. Alliance Global Corporate and Speciality, *Safety and Shipping 1912-2012 From Titanic to Costa Concordia*, Tables: World Fleet Size by Number of Ships and by Tonnage, citing

Source: Lloyd's Register Fairplay World Fleet Statistics 1900-2010 http://www.agcs.allianz.com/assets/PDFs/Reports/AGCS_safety_and_shipping_report.pdf

28. Stopford, Martin. "Will the Next Fifty Years be as Chaotic as the Last?" *Lloyd's List*, 15 May 2015, Graph, Global Fleet Development Number of Vessels 1964 -2014, http://www.lloydslist.com/ll/sector/ship-operations/article461048.ece?service=print.
29. Shukman, David. "The Largest Vessel the World has Ever Seen", *BBC News*, 20 December 2014, http://www.bbc.com/news/science-environment-30394137.
30. Wilson, Ben, *Empire of the Deep*, Note 15, pp. 553, 620, 622, 645.
31. Crucchiola, Jordan, "The New $3B *USS Zumwalt* Is a Stealthy Oddity That May Already Be a Relic", *Wired*, 15 December 2015, http://www.wired.com/2015/12/the-new-3b-uss-zumwalt-is-a-stealthy-oddity-that-may-already-be-a-relic/.
32. Cavas, Christopher P. "Pentagon Cuts LCS to 40 Ships, 1 Shipbuilder", *Defense News*, 16 December 2015, http://www.defensenews.com/story/defense/naval/2015/12/16/littoral-combat-ship-lcs-navy-budget-fighter-super-hornet-joint-strike-fighter-lockheed-martin-fincantieri-austal/77452734/.
33. Christie, Renfrew. "Opinion - A Weak Europe is not Good for the World!" *Jane's*, 5 July 2006, available at *Aktuelle Zeit*: 29. Dez 2010, 16:11, http://www.doppeladler.com/forum/viewtopic.php?f=7&t=678.
34. Stopford, Martin. "Will the Next Fifty Years be as Chaotic as the Last?", *Lloyd's List*, 15 May 2015, http://www.lloydslist.com/ll/sector/ship-operations/article461048.ece?service=print.
35. United States, Defense Advanced Research Projects Agency, *Breakthrough Technologies for national Security*, DARPA, Arlington VA, March 2015, www.darpa.mil/attachments/DARPA2015.pdf.
36. Ibid., pp.4 -5.
37. Ibid., pp.5-6.
38. United States, Office of the Press Secretary to the President, *Fact Sheet: Advancing the Rebalance to Asia and the Pacific*, 16 November 2015, https://www.whitehouse.gov/the-press-office/2015/11/16/fact-sheet-advancing-rebalance-asia-and-pacific.
39. Ibid.
40. Mishra, Raghavendra. "India and 'Indo-Pacific': Involvement rather than Entanglement", *Indian Foreign Affairs Journal*, p. 113.
41. "Russia Races Past Saudi Arabia in Tussle for Chinese Oil Market, *Bloomberg News*, 21 October 2015, http://www.bloomberg.com/news/articles/2015-10-21/russia-races-past-saudi-arabia-in-tussle-for-chinese-oil-market.
42. U.S. Energy Information Administration (EIA), *World Oil Transit Chokepoints*, 10 November 2014, http://www.eia.gov/countries/analysisbriefs/World_Oil_Transit_Chokepoints/wotc.pdf.
43. Ibid.
44. Khurana, Gurpreet S. "'*Net Security Provider' Defined*: An Analysis of India's New Maritime Strategy-2015", National Maritime Foundation, *View Point*, 23 November 2015 http://www.maritimeindia.org/View%20Profile/635838396645834619.pdf.
45. Edwards, Martin. *Roll of Honour: Royal Navy World War One British Warship Losses*, 2007, http://www.roll-of-honour.com/RoyalNavy/WarshipsLostWW1.html
46. "Royal Navy Strength and Losses", http://www.naval-history.net/WW2aBritishLosses10tables.htm.

47. "Total Axis Losses", http://www.naval-history.net/WW2aBritishLosses10tables.htm.
48. "British Ships Lost and Damaged 1st May - 12th June 1982", http://www.naval-history.net/F62-Falklands-British_ships_lost.htm ; "Units Taking Part: Royal Navy Warships", http://www.naval-history.net/F62-Falklands-British_ships_lost.htm.
49. "Germany's Disarmed Forces: Ramshackle Military at Odds with Global Aspirations", *Der Spiegel*, 30 September 2014, http://www.spiegel.de/international/germany/ramshackle-army-at-odds-with-berlin-s-global-aspirations-a-994607.html.
50. United States Government Accountability Office, *Navy Force Structure: Sustainable Plan and Comprehensive Assessment Needed to Mitigate Long-Term Risks to Ships Assigned to Overseas Homeports* Report to Congressional Committees, GAO-15-329, May 2015, http://www.gao.gov/products/GAO-15-329 pp. 56-7.
51. See, http://www.globalfirepower.com/countries-listing.asp.
52. N. A. M. Rodger, *The Command of the Ocean: A Naval History of Britain, 1649 -1815*, London, Penguin, 2004, Conclusion, pp. 575 ff.
53. N. A. M. Rodger, *The Command of the Ocean: A Naval History of Britain, 1649 -1815*, London, Penguin, 2004, pp. 577-578.
54. Ibid., p.580.
55. Ibid., p. 583.
56. Barrett,Tim. *Australian Chief of Navy Speech to Naval Warfare Officers' Association*, 30 October 2015, p. 14, http://navalinstitute.com.au/wp-content/uploads/NWOA-SPEECH.pdf.

Section II
Regional Perceptions and Approaches for Maritime Cooperative Engagements

7. Japan's Security Role in the Indo-Pacific Region

Eiichi Katahara

Introduction

At a time when the centre of gravity of international politics is shifting to the Indo-Pacific region[1] along with its unforeseen consequences, and especially given the rise of China and India as great powers and a host of global and regional non-traditional security challenges, it would be imperative that Japan—as a robust democracy and economic and maritime power with global interests—plays a major role in strengthening a rules-based international order in the twenty-first century. In particular, the evolving strategic environment at sea, characterised by competing territorial and maritime claims and the growing signs of an emerging strategic rivalry in the US–China relations, presents significant challenges for all the major powers in the region. The role of the United States remains critical in safeguarding the freedom of navigation on the seas, deterring conflict and coercion and promoting adherence to international law and standards.[2] However, the United States alone cannot secure the freedom of the seas and the broader security interests of the international community. International cooperation and collaboration would be the key to maintaining a stable maritime security order in a rapidly changing Indo-Pacific region.

This chapter discusses three questions: first, what factors are important in contributing to the maintenance of maritime security order in international society? Second, what are Japan's perceptions of maritime security issues which would focus on the emerging strategic competition among the major powers in general and on maritime security issues in the East and South China Seas in particular? Third, what would be Japan's role in ensuring maritime security in the twenty-first century Indo-Pacific region? In answering this question, it is important to discuss briefly the recent developments in Japan's security policy, focusing on the legislation for peace and security and the new Guidelines for the Japan–US Defence Cooperation. It is argued that Japan's strategy for maritime security would include the following elements: (a) increasing defence and maritime safety capabilities; (b) strengthening its alliance with the US; (c) enhancing bilateral, trilateral and multilateral security cooperation with its partners; (d) building norms, rules and mechanisms such as confidence-building measures (CBM), crisis management and arms control; (e) promoting capacity-building measures; (f) enhancing maritime domain awareness, interoperability and network centrality; (g) strengthening regional organisations such as the East Asia Summit (EAS), the ASEAN Defence Ministers' Meeting (ADMM), AMMM Plus; (h) improving decision-making structures and a whole-of-government approaches to maritime security issues and (i) strengthening multilateral cooperation to address nontraditional maritime security challenges such as humanitarian assistance/disaster relief (HA/DR), international terrorism, piracy and cyber security, including the issues related to vulnerable undersea communication cables in the oceans.

Maritime Security Order

Before discussing the maritime security issues in the Indo-Pacific region, it would be useful to consider how order is maintained in the present system of sovereign states. In his seminal work, Professor Hedley Bull emphasises the importance of three factors in providing order in the international society: common interests, rules which prescribe the pattern of behaviour that sustain common interests and institutions which make these rules effective. Bull then highlights what he describes as the institutions of international society: the balance of power, international law, diplomacy, war and the role of the great powers.[3]

In the maritime security realm, it is argued that a favourable balance of power could be crucial in maintaining an international order at sea. In more specific terms, the US has been playing a critical role in preventing the domination of the Eurasian continent by any one state or by any combination of states, thus providing a favourable balance of power.[4]

International laws and organisations, including the United Nations Convention on the Law of the Sea (UNCLOS), 'Incidents at Sea' (INCSEA) agreements such as those between the US and Russia, Western Pacific Naval Symposium (WPNS), International Court of Justice (ICJ), International Maritime Organization (IMO), etc., can fulfil significant functions in securing maritime safety, avoiding incidents at sea, resolving maritime disputes, enhancing maritime domain awareness and building confidence among the states concerned, thus contributing to the maintenance of the maritime security order. Yet, it should be noted that the efficacy and scope of these 'rules of the game' remain limited and require further strengthening.

According to Hedley Bull, diplomacy serves a number of important functions in maintaining the international order. It facilitates communication between the political leaders of states or other entities in international society. It conducts negotiations for agreements. It plays a role in gathering intelligence and information about foreign countries. It helps to minimise the effects of friction in international relations.[5] In the maritime security realm, diplomacy—both bilateral and multilateral—can serve as a principal vehicle for negotiating agreements on maritime safety and maritime/territorial disputes between states. It should also be noted that the navy can play a diplomatic role in sending some political and strategic signal to other countries.

It should also be emphasised that great powers have responsibilities and roles to play in maintaining the international norms and a rule-based international order. In the realm of maritime security, it is expected that the great powers will play crucial roles in preserving the balance of power, maintaining the freedom of navigation, the freedom of overflight and the safety of Sea Lines of Communications (SLOCs), seek to avoid or control crises in their relations with one another and to limit wars among one another, if they occur.

Given the risks of military escalation and the potentially catastrophic consequences of war, maritime and territorial disputes should be resolved by peaceful means, and military confrontation and/or war should be avoided to the greatest extent possible. Yet if deterrence fails and a war occurs, either accidentally or intentionally, it should be limited and contained, and should be terminated with the minimum costs incurred.

Japan's Perceptions of Maritime Security Issues

Japan's security perceptions reflect its position as a major maritime power with global interests, as an ally of the United States and as an increasingly proactive contributor to world peace. Although Japan has managed to deter and defend against any threat of aggression for the last 70 years since the end of the Second World War, its perceptions of physical vulnerabilities remain extremely profound. Japan is a geographically small country with densely populated cities, natural disaster-prone conditions and a rapidly aging and shrinking population; yet, it is located in a geostrategically important Northeast Asia where major powers such as China and Russia are all nuclear-armed and with significant power projection capabilities. Also, Japan is critically dependent on international trade and the SLOCs for its survival.

In more specific terms, Japan faces an array of difficult security challenges, which include the country of North Korea, armed with ballistic missiles and weapons of mass destruction, China's growing and wide-ranging military capabilities and its increasingly assertive strategic posture, the volatile situations in the Middle East and Africa, and a host of the nontraditional security issues, including cyber-attacks, natural disasters and piracy. Each of these security challenges involves the maritime dimension in general and the roles and missions for the Japanese Maritime Self-Defence Forces (JMSDF) and the Japan Coast Guard in particular. In addition to the security challenges mentioned above, there have been rising tensions in the East and South China Seas posing significant maritime security concerns for Japan and the region.

First, Tokyo is concerned about China's increasingly assertive maritime activities, including its intrusion into Japan's territorial waters and airspace. In particular, Japan deems it necessary not only to deter aggression but also to deal with the so-called 'grey-zone' situations involving the Chinese law enforcement vessels, aircraft, fishing boats and/or activists landing on the Senkaku Islands (Diaoyu islands to the Chinese) that have not yet developed into armed attacks on Japan. Indeed, we notice that there is substantial evidence of China's assertive, and in some cases coercive, behaviour in the Senkaku Islands and their adjacent waters. Beijing's promulgation of the 'Territorial Waters Law' in 1992 which included the Senkaku (or Diaoyu) Islands can be taken as China's unilateral attempt to change the status quo. Other cases in point include one in September 2010 where a collision occurred with a Chinese fishing boat; the incident of a Chinese frigate locking its firing radar on a Japanese destroyer occurred in January 2013. Since September 2012 when the Government of Japan purchased three of the Senkaku Islands from a private Japanese owner, the transfer of ownership was dramatised and misinterpreted by some countries as Japan's provocative act to change the status quo. China seized this opportunity and drastically increased its government-owned vessels and aircraft activities around the Senkaku Islands. In November 2013, it suddenly announced the establishment of an 'East China Sea Air Defence Identification Zone' that included the Senkaku Islands area within its borders. As has been observed in the International Crisis Group's study, China has been pursuing a strategy of "overlapping administration" of the Senkaku Islands and its adjacent waters with its tactics of "reactive assertiveness" vis-à-vis the Senkaku Islands.[6]

There are two important factors that complicate the Senkaku/Diaoyu Islands issue. One is the impact of domestic politics and rising nationalism on both sides. As China stands now, the Xi Jingping regime's political powerbase could become tenuous if there was to be a sudden surge of protest movement or riots triggered by mounting domestic problems such as decelerating economic growth, corruption and environmental degradation. Under these circumstances, any compromise or concessions made to Japan or any other country could undermine the Xi Jingping regime's stability. Another factor has to do with the US position on the Senkaku islands. The US government maintains that "the US does not take a position on the question of the ultimate sovereignty of the Senkaku/Diaoyu Islands". Yet, the US regards the Senkaku Islands as falling under the scope of the US–Japan security treaty and that it would oppose any attempt to undermine Japan's administration of the Islands. Indeed, President Obama put it clearly, "our treaty commitment to Japan's security is absolute, and Article 5 covers all territories under Japan's administration, including the Senkaku Islands".[7]

Despite the enduring tensions and the risks of dangerous incidents and accidents and escalation to war involving the Senkaku Islands and their adjacent waters, it would not be in the national interests of Japan, China and the US to go to war over these small uninhabited islands. Japan and China therefore agreed on an early launch of a maritime communication mechanism for avoiding and managing crises[8]. In November 2014, a significant breakthrough came when Shotaro Yachi, the head of the secretariat of Japan's National Security Council and the Chinese State Councilor Yang Jiechi jointly issued a four-point accord to improve the relationship[9] which paved the way for the subsequent Abe–Xi summit meetings. According to the document, Japan and China "recognized that they had different views as to the emergence of tense situations in recent years in the waters of the East China Sea, including those around the Senkaku Islands, and shared the view that, through dialogue and consultation, they would prevent the deterioration of the situation, establish a crisis management mechanism and avert the rise of unforeseen circumstances." Both sides also "shared the view that, by utilizing various multilateral and bilateral channels, they would gradually resume dialogue in political, diplomatic and security fields and make an effort to build a political relationship of mutual trust."[10]Although the two countries have yet to set up a crisis management mechanism at the time of writing, it appears that the Japan–China relationship is becoming stabilised. Accordingly, China's patrol activities in waters adjacent to the Senkaku Islands appear to have been reduced to 'symbolic routines'—perhaps reflecting China's appreciation of Japan's considerable restraints on the Senkaku issue. In this connection, it is worth quoting Chinese General Liu Yazhou's remark: "It is a strategic miscalculation that the Diaoyu Islands issue is the focus of the current Sino-Japanese relations."[11]

Second, China's assertive security posture, manifested in its maritime activities and land reclamation and construction of seaports and airstrips in the South China Sea, are of growing concern not only to the coastal states of the South China Sea but also to the Indo-Pacific region at large.[12] As the US Secretary of Defense Ash Carter stated on November 7, 2015:

> The United States, joins virtually everyone else in the region, in being deeply concerned about the pace and scope of land reclamation in the South China Sea, the prospect of further militarization, as well as the potential for these activities to increase the risk of miscalculation or conflict among claimant states.[13]

On October 26, the US Navy destroyer USS Lassen passed through the Spratly Islands in the First Freedom Of Navigation Operation (FONOP) in the area since 2012. The USS Lassen sailed within 12 nautical miles of the artificial islands, thus challenging China's maritime claims. China's foreign minister Wang Yi warned the United States by saying that "think twice before taking any reckless action."[14] It is possible to expect that the US FONOP could constrain China's assertive behaviour, thus mitigating the tensions and risks of military confrontation in the South China Sea. On the contrary, however, this is a worrisome prospect for worsening the situation and for heightening the risks of the US–China strategic competition in the South China Sea. The tensions in the South China Sea therefore need to be managed carefully and the disputes and disagreements should be handled by peaceful means.[15]

Third, the emerging strategic rivalry between the United States and China in the broader Indo-Pacific region is a matter of considerable concern to all the countries, because some small incident caused by miscalculation at the tactical level, say an armed clash in the South China Sea, could inadvertently escalate to a large-scale, unexpected military conflict. If Xi Jinping's 'China Dream' "is setting the stage for a prolonged period of tension between China and its neighbors, as well as for a potentially dangerous tussle for influence with a U.S. that is intent on reasserting its role as the dominant Pacific power,"[16] there is a Thucydides's Trap looming on the horizon. As Graham Allison puts it, "The defining question about global order for this generation is whether China and the United States can escape the Thucydides's Trap. ... the dangers when a rising power rivals a ruling power — as Athens challenged Sparta in ancient Greece, or as Germany did a century ago. Most such contests have ended badly, often for both nations .... When the parties avoided war, it required huge, painful adjustments in attitudes and actions on the part not just of the challenger but also the challenged." Moreover, "A risk associated with Thucydides's Trap is that business as usual—not just an unexpected, extraordinary event—can trigger large-scale conflict."[17]

Fourth, the prospect of an arms race, especially in the maritime domain, appears to be looming large in the minds of policymakers and strategists in the region. Indeed, driven by economic growth, perceived security imperatives and rising nationalism, many countries in the region continue to increase their defence budgets and build up their defence capabilities. If there is substantial evidence that an arms race—especially in the maritime domain—is in the making, it can be argued that it would stimulate further tensions and increase the prospect for conflict, because action–reaction, if not managed or controlled, could generate their own momentum.[18]

Japan's Evolving Security Policy

Japan has significantly transformed its security policy since the 1990s. Consequently, its security roles and missions have been expanded and its defence capabilities enhanced to meet the emerging threats and diverse contingencies of the twenty-first-century world.[19]

Indeed, the last two decades saw the emergence of a national consensus that Japan should play a prominent role in international peace-building and humanitarian relief operations. The success stories of the Japanese contribution to peace cooperation activities in Cambodia and East Timor helped consolidate public support for Japan's international endeavours in these fields. Some 350 SDF troops are currently engaged in peacekeeping missions in South Sudan. The SDF's non-combat logistical and reconstruction support for the US-led coalitions in Afghanistan and Iraq was also highly appreciated by the United States and its allies. The SDF has also been actively participating in multilateral security cooperation activities, including disaster relief and humanitarian operation, in response to the 2004 Indian Ocean tsunami, the peace cooperation activities in Haiti, the anti-piracy operation in the Gulf of Aden, and the Proliferation Security Initiative (PSI) exercises.

However, the question of how far Japan can go in terms of peace-building, particularly with respect to the use of force, remains highly contested. Indeed, Japan's past record has shown that its security role has been a civilian one, engaging in administration, construction, logistics, humanitarian relief and refugee matters. Until very recently, the scope of the SDF's participation in international peace-building had been very limited due to Japan's extremely restrictive interpretation of the Constitution in relation to the use of force, besides domestic political reasons. Yet given the new security policy legislation enacted last September, there is a prospect that Japan will progressively become a more proactive player engaged in peacekeeping missions that could involve the use of force by Japanese peacekeepers.

Japan's commitment to the Japan–US alliance ensures a robust US military presence in the region, thus enabling the Americans to play a central role in securing peace and stability therein. What has been taking place in recent years on this front is a gradual transformation of the Japan–US alliance in the sense that there has been a convergence of strategic objectives and interests between Japan and the United States, manifested in a series of policy documents issued through the Defence Policy Review Initiative (DPRI) in which the two governments worked together to determine how roles, missions and capabilities should be shared between the SDF and the US forces and how best to facilitate the realignment of the US forces and the military facilities and areas in Japan.

The scope of the Japan–US alliance also has been substantially expanded to include a trilateral security cooperation with both Australia and the ROK; a trilateral dialogue among the US, Japan and India; cooperation through open, multilayered regional networks and rule-making mechanisms, including the ASEAN Regional Forum (ARF), the ASEAN Defence Ministers' Meeting-Plus (ASEAN+) and the East Asia Summit (EAS).

In December 2013, the Government of Japan established its first National Security Council (NSC) as a key body tasked with national security policy decision-making and ensuring inter-ministry policy coordination. Concurrently, the Japanese government announced its first-ever National Security Strategy (NSS)[20] and the updated National Defence Program Guidelines (NDPG)[21] (the first NDPG was adopted in 1976 and it was revised in 1995, 2004 and 2010).

The new National Defence Program Guidelines for FY 2014 and beyond (2013 NDPG) adopted on December 17, 2013, represents the defence strategy of the Japanese government for the next ten years. The new NDPG builds on the policy of "proactively contributing to peace" based on the principle of international cooperation, and lays out three major policy areas: (a) Japan's own efforts; (b) strengthening of the Japan-US alliance; and (c) active promotion of security cooperation with partners and with the international community.

The fundamentals of Japan's security policy such as the exclusively defensive defence policy and the three non-nuclear principles remain intact, yet there are several notable features in the new NDPG reflecting Tokyo's changing perceptions of the strategic environment and new defence requirements. First, Japan will build the so-called 'Dynamic Joint Defence Force' which aims at enhancing the credibility of Japan's deterrent capability by promoting timely and seamless operations. This may sound ambitious, but it cannot be interpreted as involving offensive, counter-force strike capability; the Dynamic Joint Defence Force is essentially a defensive-oriented joint force placing emphasis on readiness, mobility, flexibility, sustainability, robustness and connectivity and seamless operations of intelligence, surveillance and reconnaissance (ISR) capabilities. More specifically, in terms of the defence posture, priority is given to the security of the remote southwest islands with capabilities to ensure "maritime and air superiority". The NDPG also stipulates that "the SDF will develop full amphibious capability" so as to deal with any invasion of the remote islands.

Second, deterrence and response capabilities of the Japan–US Alliance will be strengthened. Japan and the US will increase their presence in the western Pacific region and build a posture of seamless cooperation ranging from peacetime to various situations, including cooperation in responding to the so-called 'grey-zone' situations, where confrontations occur over territory, sovereignty and economic interests that stop short of war.

Third, reflecting the policy of "proactively contributing to peace" based on the principle of international cooperation, the NDPG declares that "Japan will contribute more actively than ever to ensure peace, stability and prosperity of the world." As noted already, the SDF has been actively participating in peace cooperation activities such as the UNPKO missions in South Sudan and the anti-piracy operation in the Gulf of Aden.

On April 27, 2015, Japan and the United States adopted the new Guidelines for US–Japan Defence Cooperation.[22] The new Japan–US guidelines stipulate five aims: (a) seamless, robust, flexible, and effective bilateral responses; (b) synergy across the two governments' national security policies; (c) a whole-of-government Alliance approach; (d) cooperation with regional and other partners, as well as international organizations; and (e) the global nature of the Japan–US Alliance.

There are several notable features about these new guidelines. The most significant feature is its focus on the importance of a 'seamless' defence posture. That is to say, the two countries will take measures to ensure Japan's security in all phases 'seamlessly', from peacetime to contingencies, including the 'grey-zone' situations when an armed attack against Japan is not underway. Another notable feature has to do with the establishment of a new, standing Alliance Coordination Mechanism, so as to enhance operational coordination and strengthen bilateral planning. The Alliance Coordination Mechanism would be utilised to "assess the situation; share information; and develop ways to implement the appropriate Alliance response, including flexible deterrent options, as well as actions aimed at de-escalation". Further, the guidelines highlight the global, international scope of Alliance activities, including UNPKO, HA/DR, maritime security, partner capacity building, non-combatant evacuation operations, ISR, training and exercises and logistic support. Alliance cooperation on space and cyberspace is also a new addition in the revised Japan–US guidelines.

In September 2015, the new legislation for peace and security was enacted. However, the bills turned out to be too complicated and difficult for the people to understand, and therefore failed to gain a wider public understanding and solid support. Indeed, tens of thousands Japanese citizens—young and old, men and women—led by the student group called SEALS (Student Emergency Action for Liberal Democracy) and joined by opposition lawmakers, took part in a huge demonstration protesting against what they called "war bills".

Protesters and critics, including a majority of constitutional scholars, contend that the bills are unconstitutional because of several reasons: (a) the government explanation about the legislation is insufficient and the legislation lacks public understanding and support; (b) the legislation would put the SDF personnel at greater risk; (c) Japan would become entangled in a war fought by the US and (d) the bills lack a legal basis for the SDF personnel in a combat situation because the Constitution renounces the right of belligerency by the state, meaning that the SDF personnel are all subject to civil and criminal jurisdiction because no military tribunal can be established under the Constitution.

In an effort to galvanise public support for the bills, the Abe government highlighted the worsening security environment surrounding Japan, the perceived need for Japan to make seamless responses to any situations to its security, while contributing more proactively to the peace and stability of the international community under the policy of a "proactive contribution to peace" and the importance of enhancing the deterrence of the Japan–US alliance, and at the same time deepening cooperative relations with other partners.[23] More specifically, the legislation included the following elements:

- "Limited" Execution of the Right to Collective Self-Defence: The legislation allows Japan to exercise its right to collective self-defence by deploying the SDF to respond to an attack against a country that is in a close relationship with Japan under three conditions. These involve a threat to Japan's survival, posing a clear danger in terms of fundamentally overturning its people's life, liberty and pursuit of happiness and when no other appropriate means are available, then the use of force to be limited to the minimum extent necessary.
- International Peace Support Law: A new, permanent law allows the SDF, with a prior Diet approval, to provide logistic support to the armed forces of other countries seeking collectively to secure international peace, in areas where there is no conflict underway.
- Logistic Support: The legislation allows Japan to provide logistic support to the US and other countries engaged in operations in

situations which have an "important influence" on Japan's security. This expands the scope of the so-called SIASJ (Situations in Areas Surrounding Japan) and clarifies that there are no geographical constraints. It also expands the scope of logistic support by allowing the provision of services and supplies, including ammunition, to the US and other military forces.

- Peacekeeping Operations: The legislation not only allows Japanese troops to protect civilians but also to rescue the troops of other countries participating in peacekeeping missions and it adopts the rules of engagement (ROE) for the use of weapons during peacekeeping operations. It also enables Japan to participate in internationally coordinated peace and security operations outside the UNPKO framework.

More specifically, what kinds of military actions would the laws allow the SDF to conduct? One media analysis succinctly outlines the key points in this regard as:

- Japan would be able to provide logistic support to South Korea if the North were to invade and Tokyo was asked by the ROK to support; though, it would still be against the Constitution to send Japanese troops to fight on Korean soil.
- It would be legal for Japan to shoot down a North Korean missile headed for the US. Currently, North Korea has to threaten Japan in order to justify its shooting its missiles down; although, North Korea is thought to be several years away from being able to hit the mainland US targets.
- Military action to keep the shipping lanes secure, such as minesweeping—even in an active conflict zone—might be allowed if the restriction on shipping was severe enough to constitute a threat to Japan's survival.
- Armed involvement in hostage rescues would also become possible.
- Regional limits on the Japanese military support for the US and other foreign armed forces would also be eliminated.[24]

As has been described, there has been a marked progress in Japan's security policy under the Abe government. Japan's National Security Strategy (NSS), the new National Defence Program Guidelines (NDPG), the new Guidelines for the US–Japan Defence Cooperation and the legislation for peace and security taken together would be a substantial step forward, if not "a big, big, fundamental, improvement in the way in which we do things together", as Assistant Secretary of Defense David Shear has opined.[25]

Taking these changes into consideration, it is posited that Japan's strategy for maritime security would include the following elements:

- Increasing defence and maritime safety capabilities to deter aggression and coercion by developing the SDF's 'dynamic joint force' and enhancing the Japanese Coast Guard's capabilities;
- Strengthening its alliance with the US in order to deter aggression and coercion by increasing the US military presence and upgrading the alliance roles, missions and capabilities—including a strengthening of the ISR and amphibious operation capabilities, developing the alliance roles in AirSea Battle (ASB) such as tactical air operations, ASW, air defence and possibly sea mining capabilities—and developing the Japan–US joint crisis-management and crisis-prevention mechanisms, including the mechanisms for de-escalation and escalation controls;
- Enhancing bilateral, trilateral and multilateral security cooperation with its partners, including India, China, Australia, Russia, ROK, ASEAN and the EU. It would be in the interests of Japan and China to fundamentally stabilise and improve the Japan–China relations through a new modus vivendi vis-à-vis the Senkaku Islands and the comprehensive promotion of a "mutually beneficial relationship based on common strategic interests";
- Building norms, rules and mechanisms such as confidence-building measures (CBM), crisis management and arms control. Japan could play both political and diplomatic roles in institutionalising and operationalising the "three principles on the rule of law at sea". As Prime Minister Abe put it, "The first principle is that states shall make their claims based on international law. The second is that States shall not use force or coercion in trying to drive their claims. The third principle is that States shall seek to settle disputes by peaceful means. So to reiterate this, it means making claims that are faithful in light of international law, not resorting to force or coercion, and resolving all disputes through peaceful means."[26] Japan's diplomatic support for the ASEAN in the SCS Code of Conduct (CoC) should be continued. International laws and institutions, including the Convention on the International Regulations for Preventing Collisions at Sea (COLREGs), the WPNS Code for Un-alerted Encounters at Sea (CUES) and arms control measures such as Incidents at Sea Agreement should be enhanced. An effective Japan–China crisis management mechanism and possibly a Japan-US-China trilateral crisis management mechanism should be established.
- Promoting capacity-building measures directed at the ASEAN countries, including the provision of patrol vessels to Indonesia, the Philippines and Vietnam;

- Enhancing maritime domain awareness, interoperability and network centrality, including the possible use of automatic identification system (AIS) satellites for maritime domain awareness;
- Strengthening regional organisations such as the East Asian Summit (EAS), the ASEAN Defense Ministers' Meeting (ADMM) and the ADMM Plus. In particular, an Experts Working Group (EWG) on Maritime Security should be utilised to promote maritime security cooperation such as information-sharing and joint exercises and training.
- Improving decision-making structures and whole-of-government approaches to maritime security issues;
- Strengthening multilateral cooperation for addressing nontraditional maritime security challenges such as HA/DR, international terrorism, piracy and cyber security, including the issues related to vulnerable undersea communication cables in the oceans.

Conclusion

Japan would play a major role in strengthening a rule-based international order in the twenty-first century world. The time has come for Japan to get its political, economic and strategic fundamentals right and face up to the strategic challenges in the current century. Japan needs to increase its comprehensive national power and update its national security strategy, articulate its national interests and the means to protect and enhance them. In view of the lessons drawn from the experience of the 3/11 disaster, it requires a strong political leadership, transparent governance and comprehensive national strategies for an effective crisis management.

Given Japan's demographic challenges, its financial and manpower constraints and the time-honoured pacifism of the Japanese rooted in their experience of hunger, devastation and suffering during the Asia-Pacific War as well as the lessons from the wartime past, even if Japan becomes a 'normal power' at some point in the future, it will remain a cautious, careful and prudent security policy player. It is important to avoid great-power strategic competition and confrontation and conflicts need to be avoided at all costs. It would also be imperative for the major powers including the US, Japan, India, China and the middle and small powers in the region to share the responsibilities in shaping a new security order in the Indo-Pacific region.

Notes

1. The concept of 'Indo-Pacific' is not being widely used in Japan except when it comes to addressing security issues related to India and the Indian Ocean. In this paper, the term 'Indo-Pacific region' is used to highlight the increasing relevance of the concept in addressing maritime security issues in the broader Indo-Pacific region encompassing the entire Asia-Pacific region, the Indian Ocean and the countries littoral to these oceans. Prime Minister Shinzo Abe, in his speech delivered at the Indian Parliament in August 2007, placed considerable emphasis on the confluence of the Pacific and the Indian Oceans, as he put it: "The Pacific and the Indian Oceans are now bringing about a 'dynamic coupling as seas' of freedom and prosperity. A 'broader Asia' that broke away geographical boundaries is now beginning to take on a distinct form". See Prime Minister Shinzo Abe, "Confluence of the Two Seas", Parliament of the Republic of India, 22 August 2007, http://www.mofa.go.jp/region/asia-paci/pmv0708/speech-2.html. In the joint statement titled 'Japan and India Vision 2025 Special Strategic and Global Partnership: Working Together for Peace and Prosperity of the Indo-Pacific Region and the World' issued on December 12, 2015, the concept of 'Indo-Pacific', not the traditional 'Asia-Pacific', is used. See, http://www.mofa.go.jp/s_sa/sw/in/page3e_000432.html.
2. U.S. Department of Defense, *Asia-Pacific Maritime Security Strategy*, August 2015, http://www.defense.gov/Portals/1/Documents/pubs/NDAA%20A-P_Maritime_SecuritY_Strategy-08142015-1300-FINALFORMAT.PDF
3. Bull, Hedley. *The Anarchical Society: A Study of Order in World Politics*. New York: Columbia University Press, 1977.
4. See, for example, Layne, Christopher. *The Peace of Illusions: American Grand Strategy from 1940 to the Present*. Ithaca: Cornell University Press, 2006, and; Brzezinski, Zbigniew. *The Grand Chessboard: American Primacy and Its Geostrategic Imperatives*. New York, NY: BasicBooks, 1997.
5. Bull, *The Anarchical Society,* Note 3, pp. 162-183.
6. International Crisis Group, "Dangerous Waters: China-Japan Relations on the Rocks", *Asia Report* No 245, 8 April 2013, http://www.crisisgroup.org/~/media/Files/asia/north-east-asia/245-dangerous-waters-china-japan-relations-on-the-rocks.pdf.
7. Joint Press Conference with President Obama and Prime Minister Abe of Japan, 24 April 2014, https://www.whitehouse.gov/the-press-office/2014/04/24/joint-press-conference-president-obama-and-prime-minister-abe-japan .
8. See, for example, *Kyodo News*, 5 November 2015, "Japan, China agree on early launch of maritime communication mechanism", https://english.kyodonews.jp/news/2015/11/382707.html.
9. Japan Ministry of Foreign Affairs, "Regarding Discussions toward Improving Japan-China Relations", 7 November 2014, http://www.mofa.go.jp/a_o/c_m1/cn/page4e_000150.html. For the Chinese version, see *Xinhuanet*, "China, Japan rReach Four-Point Agreement on Ties", 7 November 2014, http://news.xinhuanet.com/english/china/2014-11/07/c_133772952.htm.
10. Ibid.
11. Yazhou, Liu. "Diaoyu Islands and Sino-Japanese Relations", *China Military Online*, 14 October 2015, http://english.chinamil.com.cn/news-channels/2015-10/14/content_6722816.htm.

12. For Japan's perception of this problem, see Japan Ministry of Defence, "China's Activities in the South China Sea", 28 July 2015, http://www.mod.go.jp/j/approach/surround/pdf/ch_d-act_20150728e.pdf .
13. Secretary of Defense Ash Carter, Remarks on "Strategic and Operational Innovation at a Time of Transition and Turbulence" at Reagan Defense Forum, 7 November 2015, http://www.defense.gov/News/News-Transcripts/Transcript-View/Article/628147/remarks-on-strategic-and-operational-innovation-at-a-time-of-transition-and-tur.
14. Cooper, Helen. "Challenging Chinese Claims, U.S. Sends Warships Near Artificial Island Chain", *The New York Times*, 26 October 2015, http://www.nytimes.com/2015/10/27/world/asia/challenging-chinese-claims-us-sends-warship-near-artificial-island-chain.html?_r=0.
15. For an analysis of the South China Sea disputes, see Raine,Sarah and Christian Le Miere. *Regional Disorder: The South China Sea Disputes*. London: IISS, 2013.
16. Page, Jeremy. "For Xi, a 'China Dream' of Military Power", *The Wall Street Journal*, 13 March 2013, http://www.wsj.com/articles/SB10001424127887324128504578348774040546346 .
17. Allison, Graham. "The Thucydides Trap: Are the U.S. and China Headed for War?" *The Atlantic*, 24 September 2015.
18. Till, Geoffrey. *Asia's Naval Expansion: An Arms Race in the Making?* London: IISS, 2012; Ball, Desmond, "Northeast Asia: Tensions and Action-Reaction Dynamics", Working Paper, International Institute of Strategic Studies-Asia, 25 January 2012.
19. For an excellent exposition of Japan's Maritime SDF, see Takai, Tomohisa. "Japan Maritime Self-Defense Force in the New Maritime Era", *Hatou*, November 2008, http://www.mod.go.jp/msdf/navcol/SSG/topics-column/images/c-030/c-030_eng.pdf .
20. Government of Japan, 'National Security Strategy,' 17 December 2013, http://www.cas.go.jp/jp/siryou/131217anzenhoshou/nss-e.pdf.
21. See Government of Japan, "National Defense Program Guidelines for FY 2014 and beyond", 17 December 2013, http://www.mod.go.jp/j/approach/agenda/guideline/2014/pdf/20131217_e2.pdf.
22. See Government of Japan, "Guidelines for U.S.-Japan Defense Cooperation", 27 April 2015, http://www.mofa.go.jp/files/000078188.pdf.
23. See Government of Japan, "Japan's Legislation for Peace and Security", November 2015, http://www.mofa.go.jp/files/000080671.pdf.
24. BBC News, "Japan to allow military role overseas in historic move", 18 September 2015, http://www.bbc.com/news/world-asia-34287362 .
25. Shear, David. "New U.S.-Japan Defense Guidelines transform the Alliance into 'Seamless and Global'", *The Asahi Shimbun*, 29 April 2015, http://ajw.asahi.com/article/views/opinion/AJ201504290004 .
26. Prime Minister Shinzo Abe, Shangri-La Dialogue 2014 Keynote Address, http://www.iiss.org/en/events/shangri%20la%20dialogue/archive/2014-c20c/opening-remarks-and-keynote-address-b0b2/keynote-address-shinzo-abe-a787.

8. Globalisation, International Liberalism and the Maritime Cooperation Nexus

K. Raja Menon

Fleet reviews date back to the fifteenth century and used to be the symbols of naval power. That tradition has been modified to International Fleet Reviews, which are grand peaceful exercises that are non-threatening in character. The International Fleet Review (IFR), hosted by India in 2016, collected a significant international audience and the participation by ships and delegations from a large number of countries which is indicative of the success of the maritime strategic outreach effort of the Indian Navy.

Navies and maritime strategy have clearly come a long way through the centuries, and particularly in the last hundred years. It needs no reminding that it was just over a hundred years ago that Alfred Thayer Mahan was putting pen to paper to write his famous treatise[1] on what navies need to do to win wars and conflicts, setting off many authors to write on the same subject.

The naval fraternity can best be described as one belonging to the profession of arms which are also the instruments of state of respective nations. Yet, it is in the spirit of peace and goodwill that the majority of the global community has collected for the IFR, to honour the profession of arms—and each other— in this grand event. Major maritime and naval developments have taken place over the last hundred years. Whereas the beginning of this period saw a proliferation of naval literature on how to win wars, the discourse today is mostly about ideas on the use of navies as instruments of foreign policy and cooperation.

This transformation from the focus on war-fighting to enhanced maritime cooperation needs s brief explanation. After Admiral Mahan wrote his great works, Sir Julian Corbett, the British maritime historian, emphasised that while maritime superiority is a precondition for victory, man is essentially a land animal.[2] Corbett went on to argue that the great affairs of nations are decided on land by decisions or treaties that are invariably arrived at by the 'boots on the ground'—to use a modern term—with some notable exceptions, such as the ceremony on board the

USS Missouri in 1945 when General MacArthur signed the surrender of Japan.

The first half of the twentieth century produced some of the best writings on maritime warfare in a strategic sense, and this is not surprising considering that two world wars occurred in such a short space of time. Europe today has become one entity and it is seventy years since most of the European navies participated in a full-fledged war. Not surprisingly, many of these naval forces have been involved in low-end functions like the anti-piracy patrol and humanitarian assistance necessary to meet the refugee crisis arising from the war in Syria.

It is worth recalling two continental European writers who are not much read or quoted these days. The first is the French Admiral Raoul Castex who spent the First World War patrolling the Mediterranean in what he perceived to be a sideshow of the war. This made him question the role of navies in what were predominantly continental wars[3]—a subject close to this author since it happens to be the title of his first work, *Maritime Strategy and Continental Wars*. The utility of navies in land-centric conflicts continues to be an interesting subject. Many navies have found themselves in the same conundrum, just as the Indian Navy did in its first war with Pakistan in 1965, when it received very ambiguous orders from the government 'not' to widen the war.

The second European writer worth recalling is the German Admiral Wegener who wrote a book on the suggested maritime strategy for a geographically disadvantaged country like Germany that harboured great maritime aspirations.[4] Admiral Wegener suggested that if such a country was to get into a total war, then the army would have to be used to change the country's geography into a more favourable one. Admiral Wegener was passed over by the high command in favour of Admiral Raeder just before the Second World War, but Raeder found Wegener's prescriptions to be most appropriate. Without getting into the minutiae of World War II history, an article from the US Naval War College suggested that China, for instance, is geographically disadvantaged since it only has a Pacific Ocean coastline, whereas its strategic sea lanes are all in the Indian Ocean.[5] This of course is true and explains why some countries have been slow to accept that the 'One Belt One Road' may have more than just geo-economic benefits. Quite clearly, for China to become an Indian Ocean power, there would have to be some rearrangement of geography, that is, of course, assuming that China must become an Indian Ocean power to protect its strategic SLOCs which cannot, for instance, leave their protection to the international system, as the Japanese have done all these years.

Navies all over the world are aware that cooperation with other navies is one of their tasks, but all acknowledge that war-fighting remains the primary purpose of fighting navies. This chapter does not attempt to stand that theory upon its head, but attempts to point out that war-fighting will increasingly become a rare occupation, particularly in light of what Francis Fukuyama wrote in his famous work, *The End of History and the Last Man*.[6] Fukuyama's thesis is that liberal democracy is some kind of an end point for humankind and that since the French Revolution there is an inexorable, if slow, movement by countries and governments to move towards liberal democracy. He does not indicate that there are no autocracies and dictatorships in the world, but if one looks at the world in say 1800, and the world in 2000, there is a noticeable movement towards liberal democracy (Figure 1).

Figure 1: The Impulse for Democratisation since the Eighteenth Century

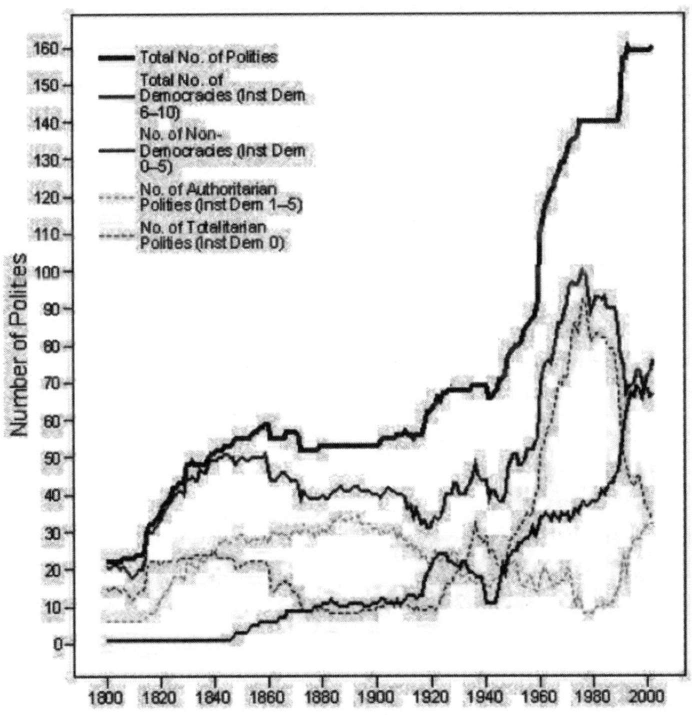

Source: Mikael Sandberg, *Soft Power, World System Dynamics, and Democratization* (2011)

Further, empirical evidence by proponents of the Democratic Peace theory points out that liberal participative governments do not engage in a clash of arms with nations with similar political structures.[7] The point for emphasis is that there is a gradual but inevitable acceptance of the growing futility of wars as a means of solving disputes. Some may feel cynical about this theoretical logic when witnessing some recent developments like those in Ukraine, Yemen, Libya, Syria and Iraq. These are indeed trouble spots and Fukuyama fully acknowledges that the movement towards liberal democracy is a stuttering one with many hold ups, speed breakers and reversals. However, he also postulates that instances like Iraq and Yemen are merely exceptions to the broad flow of events towards democratisation and not the main trend itself. As a convert to the ideas propagated in *The End of History*, I would like the readership to be convinced that over a century of human history, countries will increasingly give up authoritarian regimes and adopt the end point of history which is liberal democracy—perhaps not in the immediate future, but eventually. Thomas PM Barnett has suggested that the countries of the world could be divided into two:[8] the first being the core world—those which have already converted into liberal democracies—and the other the peripheral world, which have countries with governments that are unrepresentative of the people, have no declared human rights and no compunctions in leading their countries into war frequently.

The question that arises is that whether in the region under discussion—the Asia-Pacific or as what some now refer in its expanded avatar as the Indo-Pacific—there are any countries in what has been described as the peripheral world, with a tendency towards declaring war as an instrument of policy. Clearly, North Korea is an extreme example of a country in the peripheral world, but it is not important to see which are and which aren't. Europe, for instance, has strict criteria for joining the EU, which inter alia includes a democratically elected government, but there are no similar barriers in Asia for joining any grouping. Nevertheless, it can be averred with some certainty that it has been some decades since Asia witnessed any major armed conflict—perhaps the last full-fledged war was the Indo-Pakistan war of 1971 and that was 45 years ago. These propositions further strengthen Fukuyama's thesis and that the incidence of wars will decline in the years to come as countries increasingly adopt liberal democracy as the ideal form of government.

This may not be encouraging news for the younger generations which have joined a profession of arms for fame and glory, but the navy will still be an interesting career option even if there are no more wars to be fought, or only the occasional skirmish to satisfy young blood. So, in the hierarchy of tasks for the navy, it may sound as a sorry dampener but is a hard reality about the raison d'etre on the opening (foundational) task of armed forces which is war-fighting. This is not to say that war-fighting will become any the less important. Navies will continue to prepare for wars (deterrence) as their primary task, but it has to be accepted that in the core world, it may well be that a couple of generations of naval officers may never see any conflict although they will be fully prepared for that eventuality.

This brings to the fore the other tasks that navies do remarkably well in all circumstances. The first is naval diplomacy; everyone is aware of Oliver Cromwell's famous statement that "a man o' war is the best ambassador". The US Navy has carried this farther to T-shirts bearing the slogan "90,000 tons of diplomacy" to describe their strike aircraft carriers. The term is not understood by the layman but among professionals, naval diplomacy can achieve many foreign policy goals short of war. In fact, the coming on stage of major powers in the world has been accompanied by high levels of naval diplomacy, as witnessed by the rise of Great Britain in the eighteenth and nineteenth centuries and by the rise of the United States in the early twentieth century—particularly during the presidency of Theodore Roosevelt. This is also reflected today in the rise of China, accompanied by a growth of its maritime power. Naval diplomacy can achieve a great deal short of open conflict; the only problem is that those theorists who have written on maritime conflict outnumber those who have weighed in on naval diplomacy, like James Cable and Ken Booth.[9]

Naval diplomacy represents the use of navies to achieve geopolitical goals short of the use of force. There are many examples of the navy not having to fire a shot in order to influence events on land favourably. In many ways, the use of naval diplomacy comes somewhere in between Joseph Nye's definition of 'soft power'[10] and the full-fledged use of warships in a 'hard power' mode, in an environment punctuated by the declining utility of war among liberal democracies. From the earlier analysis during the course of this chapter, it emerges that the practice of naval diplomacy is going to grow during the long years of peace that many expect will reign. The usual practices of flying the flag and showing presence are fully compatible with the principles of exerting soft power.

Naval diplomacy, as practised by nations today, assuages the insecurity of all nations about the safety of their Sea Lines of Communication (SLOCs). In this, the United States has set the lead in asking the other navies to join the cooperation venture of a 1000- ship navy proposition, floated about a decade ago. What could the nations of Asia do, for instance, to reassure China that the Malacca Dilemma is a creation of Beijing's own imagination, since one constantly comes across Chinese scholarship on this subject?[11] Should the navies of all nations be equally responsible for the smooth flow of the world's strategic cargoes, particularly the hydrocarbons? Is it necessary for the nations to start thinking of escorting and convoying in peacetime, merely because they have vulnerabilities like everyone else? Some authors have spoken about the benefits to the world of the US Navy possessing what is called 'hegemonic stability' where the hegemon seeks a peaceful status quo of the world order and commercial peace. Theodore Roosevelt allegedly kicked off this idea by the round-the-world cruise of the Great White Fleet in 1907, but today the US Navy's worldwide deployment is routine and quite unremarkable.

In the Asia-Pacific, or the Indo-Pacific, some questions have been raised about the practical legitimacy of the Indian Navy operating in the South China Seas while the Peoples Liberation Army (Navy) [PLAN] operates increasingly in the Indian Ocean. These should not be seen as alarming developments because that is exactly what navies do—operate in the blue or distant waters as they become more capable. Ken Booth was more specific in describing the seven characteristics of warships that make them so practical to the conduct of naval diplomacy. Booth also divided naval diplomacy into 'naval power politics' and 'naval influence politics'—a subtle but important distinction which is not only difficult to define but even more difficult to comprehend for an ab initio readership.[12] However, if one was to accept Fukuyama's theory about the end of history as also the declining utility of war, it becomes apparent that Booth's idea of 'naval influence politics' is going to be of increasing relevance. Another great strategist who emphasised influence politics was Admiral Gorshkov. His work was largely addressed to a domestic audience and continuously used examples from Western naval history to reiterate that the use of navies in peacetime for the purpose of exercising influence was necessary for a nation to be a great power. He emphasised that it was not enough for navies to defend coastlines as the Soviet Marshals thought and kept pointing out that NATO was an alliance of maritime states.

Today, global politics is being largely driven by the rise of China and the possible overtaking of the US as the country with the largest GDP, at least in purchasing power terms. The financial centre of gravity is already shifting to the East and the moot point being how long it will be before the maritime centre of gravity also shifts in the same direction. Perhaps this development may manifest itself in a few decades, but using the propositions reiterated earlier, it could be argued that it would be a peaceful shift. The Chinese keep stressing that their rise will be peaceful. Certainly, ever since the border agreement on peace and tranquillity in 1993, there have been no violent incidents on the world's longest deputed border, i.e. the Sino-Indian one. During these years of peace, navies can continue to jockey for influence, as

Geoffrey Till has pointed out in his chapter in this book about the Indian Navy's limited deployment in the Pacific in 2007.

In conclusion, it may well be averred that in the years of peace which stretch before us, naval war colleges and other similar military institutions will probably have to put a bit more emphasis on authors like James Cable, Ken Booth and Sergei Gorshkov[13] who wrote more about the diplomatic use of navies than how to fight wars. Many operations have touched upon the great successes of the navies in operations other than war and in humanitarian work, as exemplified by the Somalia patrol and the relief work after the 2004 Indian Ocean Tsunami. It is quite certain that greater successes await navies in the future in this line of work, also in cooperation with other navies. Of course navies cannot deploy themselves independently—they need government (political and diplomatic) approval—but the readiness, willingness and enthusiasm is purely of naval origin, and the best aspect of naval works is that they leave no footprint behind. There are many stories from the Indian Navy of lightning decisions given and taken over the telephone; all navies have such stories. As long as the navy and the diplomats are on the same page, much can be achieved without red tape. Navies with an ancient history are fortunate in this respect for they are more likely to have well-oiled decision-making processes to act on humanitarian and diplomatic grounds at short notice.

Notes

1. Mahan, A. T. *The Influence of Sea Power Upon History, 1660*-1783, Boston: Little, Brown and Company, 1890.
2. Corbett, Julian Stafford. *Some Principles of Maritime Strategy*. Annapolis, Md: Naval Institute Press, 1988 edn, p.14.
3. Castex, Raoul, and Eugenia C. Kiesling. *Strategic Theories*. Annapolis, Md: Naval Institute Press, 1994.
4. Wegener, Wolfgang. *Die Seestrategie Des Weltkrieges ... Mit Einer Ubersichtsskizze*. 1929. The English translation was published as Wegener, Wolfgang. *The Naval Strategy of the World War*. Annapolis, Md: Naval Institute Press, 1989.
5. Hansen, Kenneth P. "Raeder Versus Wegener: Conflict in German Naval Strategy", *Naval War College Review*. Vol. 58, no. 4, (Autumn 2005), pp. 85-89.
6. Fukuyama, Francis. *The End of History and the Last Man*. New York: Free Press, 1992.
7. See generally, Russett, Bruce M., and John R. Oneal. *Triangulating Peace: Democracy, Interdependence, and International Organizations*. New York: Norton, 2001 and; Russett, Bruce M. *Grasping the Democratic Peace Principles for a Post-Cold War World*. Princeton, N.J.: Princeton University Press, 1995.
8. Barnett, Thomas P. M. *The Pentagon's New Map: War and Peace in the Twenty-First Century*. New York: G.P. Putnam's Sons, 2004.

9. See, Cable, James. *Diplomacy at Sea*. Annapolis, Md: Naval Institute Press, 1985 and Cable, James. *The Political Influence of Naval Force in History*. Basingstoke, England: Macmillan, 1998. Also, Booth, Ken. *Navies and Foreign Policy*. London: Croom Helm, 1977.
10. Nye, Joseph S. *Soft Power: The Means to Success in World Politics*. New York: Public Affairs, 2004.
11. Zhang, Zhong Xiang, "China's Energy Security, the Malacca Dilemma and Responses", *Energy Policy*, Volume 39, Issue 12, December 2011, pp. 7612–7615 and; Shaofeng, Chen. "China's Self-Extrication from the "Malacca Dilemma and Implications", *International Journal of China Studies*, Vol. 1, No. 1, January 2010, pp. 1-24.
12. Booth, Note 9, pp. 27-29.
13. Gorshkov, Sergeĭ Georgievich. *The Sea Power of the State*. Annapolis, Md: Naval Institute Press, 1979.

9. Cooperative Maritime Engagement in the Indo-Pacific Region

Geoffrey Till

To address the issue of cooperative engagement in the Indo-Pacific Region there first needs to be an exercise in the 'naming of parts'. What does "maritime engagement" actually mean? 'Engagement' is a neutral word, which covers a range of contingencies. At one end, it applies to two people 'engaged' to be married and at the other to military forces seeking to destroy each other. It clearly has both cooperative and competitive connotations; the former conducive to peace, the latter potentially leading to conflict. Because, what happens anywhere in the system naturally tends to affect everywhere. Globalisation means that all externally functioning states are engaged with each other; very often this is regardless of how activist they are internationally. The requirement then is for cooperative engagement to be encouraged and competitive engagement discouraged.

There seem to be three closely inter-connected dimensions to maritime engagements in the Indo-Pacific: substantive ('what they engage about'), behavioural ('how they engage') and institutional ('where they engage'). In all three dimensions, the more cooperative the engagement the better will be the chance of peace and prosperity in any particular region.

Maritime Engagement: The Substantive Policy Angle

Almost by definition, substantive engagement is a matter of what is sometimes—if misleadingly—known as 'grand strategy'; it is about the interaction of national policy objectives, about the 'ends' that governments seek to attain. In the Indo-Pacific Region there is an encouraging supply of substantive issues, which naturally tend to draw the nations together into collaborative relationships.

The most obvious perhaps is the growth of maritime economic interdependency and the developing common need to defend the sea-based trading system on which the peace, prosperity and regime survival of all nations depends. Economic interdependence amongst the region's major players is steadily growing. Concerns about the impact of some troubling aspects of China's economic development remind us that everyone has a critical stake in the outcome. Likewise, any disruption of the safe and timely passage of merchant ships on which the system depends would adversely affect everyone. Dealing with threats to it is an essentially cooperative endeavour. That is why the international counter-piracy mission off Somalia has been such a benign development, and such maritime cooperation should be encouraged more widely.

Much the same can be said about the increasingly recognised need to combat the illegal trade in drugs, the trafficking of human beings and of course global warming and to guard against their consequences for the stability of the system. All these are likewise in the common interest and painfully obvious to everyone. The spread of international terrorism also represents a common threat, since it increasingly appears that nowhere is safe, and that instability in one part of the system adversely affects all the other parts. Although different nations clearly have differing priorities in responding to such threats, there is much substantive agreement about the need to contain them and where there is a significant maritime element to the problem, for their navies to work together.

This is true both of predictable and unpredictable contingencies. The campaign against the illegal trade in drugs, for example, is most unlikely to be completely 'won' in the foreseeable future, if ever. That makes it a permanent fixture in the contingencies that navies do and will have to meet. Disasters, on the other hand, are much less predictable–especially in terms of time, place and nature. Preparing for them calls for the kind of advance and collective planning which means that when disasters strike, navies will be able to exploit the habits of fraternity to cooperate 'when', 'how' and 'where' needed.

The planning and implementation of responses to such challenges to the system have to be continuous. This not only helps preserve the system, it also improves relations between maritime states. Their navies cooperate better— operationally and tactically. Strategically and politically, such multinational naval action against common threats reinforces international togetherness. It mitigates tensions and helps put other things into proportion.

However, there are other 'things'—issues where national policy interests clash and where national action at sea—or maritime engagement which quickly become competitive, and sometimes dangerously so. The current levels of tension in the East and South China Seas illustrate the point. It would be naïve to ignore the future possibility of dangerously increasing tensions between India and Pakistan, between the US and China, between the two Koreas, Japan and China and so on. In such a maritime area as the Indo-Pacific region, it is hardly surprising that many of these issues should themselves be of a maritime nature. For this reason, naval planners throughout the region feel they have a duty to 'engage' in a worst-case analysis and to produce as strong a force as they can in order to minimise strategic risks. Inevitably, this produces security dilemmas where one country's defensive measures seem to justify its neighbours' responses in an endless chain of actions and reactions leading to a retreat from collaborative engagement and a slide into heightened tensions and a destabilising arms race. The complex relationship between the nuclear deterrent policies of India and Pakistan is one very obvious example of this.

While it is true that such countries when locked in particular disputes—say, over who owns what in the South or East China seas—still have much in common, the substantial issues that they do *not* have in common will tend to be intractable, and very possibly beyond solution. All too often, we imagine that every problem has a solution. In many cases, they do not. Nations have to sit on the shore and wait for the breeze— or in other words, wait until radical shifts in the context make the problem go away, as the end of the Cold War suddenly made the fiendishly difficult issue of Berlin disappear. Until such changes occur, the differences need to be lived with and the very limited prospect of cooperative engagement in those particular areas accepted realistically. The substance of the issue may not be changeable, but its effects might be moderated by changes in behaviour.

Maritime Engagement: The Behavioural Angle

With this we step from the grand-strategic level of national policy where objectives or 'ends' are defined down to the operational levels where strategy, ways and means come into play. This is less a matter of policy, more one of ways and means—of strategy, and at all levels. Some engagement behaviours contribute to, rather than make more difficult, stable and acceptably harmonious relationships at sea and elsewhere; others do not. It should be helpful, then, to consider behavioural engagement at two levels: the operational (ways) and the tactical (means).

The Operational Level

Throughout the Indo-Pacific region, there are a large number of differing national maritime objectives at sea which cannot easily be reconciled, but which nonetheless have to be accepted indefinitely. This being so, it seems important operationally to insulate other areas of policy agreement and cooperation from the potentially toxic effect of these outstanding maritime disputes as much as possible.

An obvious example of the diplomatic dangers of the alternative approach of 'cross-wiring' rather than insulating generally benign relationships from particular intractable issues at sea has been demonstrated by tensions over the South and East China Seas. In general, all parties to these disputes have a common interest in a cooperative economic context that is produced by a shared interest in the effective workings of the sea-based trading system. However, this was damaged when China succumbed to the temptation to make use of its economic levers of power when dealing with Japan over the East China Sea by making access to its rare earth minerals difficult some time ago,[1] or suddenly discovering that there was something wrong with the Philippine bananas at the time of the squabble over the Scarborough shoal. These acts turned economic dependency into political leverage and violated the *seikei bunri* principle in Japan's post-war foreign policy of separating politics and economics in the conduct of international relations. These actions can surely be seen as a bad idea firstly because they reduce the compensatory effect of close economic relationships in otherwise difficult times, and secondly raise security concerns about allowing such economic dependencies to develop in the first place. Instead, it would be in China's interest and in everyone else's too to *encourage* economic interdependency on the basis of the old argument of the Manchester School that the more nations trade together, generally the less they fight.[2]

This experience rebounded on China in several ways. Firstly, it encouraged Japan to seek other sources of these rare earth minerals and for countries like Vietnam and India to develop them. These burgeoning economic relationships encouraged a further coming together of these countries politically in ways that were almost certainly unwelcome in Beijing. Secondly, such experience has had its effect on attitudes towards China's One Belt One Road (OBOR) project. OBOR, the Chinese say, along with the twenty-first-century Maritime Silk Road (MSR), should not be seen as tools of geopolitics; instead, they are to be seen as an opportunity, not a threat.[3] Thus, Premier Li Keqiang said:

> We stand ready to work with other countries to boost economic growth, deepen international cooperation and promote world peace through developing the ocean, and we strive to build a peaceful, cooperative and harmonious ocean.[4]

However, the twenty-first century MSR could have at least some 'hegemonic' connotations (just as did the famous voyages of the fifteenth century so often regarded as a model of non-confrontational maritime endeavour).[5] Even though it is clearly preferable to the 'deliberate use of force' in the operational pursuit of policy objectives, economic leverage of such nature while tactically effective often turns out to operationally unwise in the long run.

Interestingly, though, there still remains the question of how regional countries should respond to the engagement issues involved in the OBOR. One obvious temptation for the countries having doubts about the operational consequences of this project for them would be to have nothing to do with it, i.e. to refuse to engage with it. This would probably be unwise. There is a strong alternative argument that suggests that cautious engagement would be the best way of finding out what the project actually means; to ensure that the economics make sense and that as much as possible the dependencies go both ways in a manner that makes it more difficult for any of the parties to exploit them strategically. It may bind the countries involved more closely together, and also, if the Manchester School is right, then the long-term consequence of this consequence might well be generally benign.

The Tactical Level

Tactical engagement—the means—is clearly important also for this is often where accidents happen and when unintended consequences follow. Tactical actions at sea which endanger life and violate the basic rules of the road have a high risk of being counterproductive. It may be better to direct high-pressure water at the bridge and communications equipment of the other side in some standoff at sea than to shoot at him but it is still inherently dangerous. It could easily result in the victim either at sea or ashore losing control of the situation or doing something escalatory. It will often poison relationships afterwards as well, affecting the perceptions and assumptions the parties have of each other. In perilous situations (as potentially all situations at sea are), control and restraint should be at a premium and competition in risk-taking frowned upon.

The wisdom of making the tactical engagement as constructive as possible applies just as much to talks about methods of controlling incidents at sea. Cooperation in formal talks and informal exchanges over the establishment of hotlines or talks on the avoidance of incidents at sea should, for example, surely *not* be suspended when things get difficult. Logically, this is just when such measures are at their most important. Participating in such negotiations and the effective implementation of their outcomes should surely be regarded as the natural default position, rather than a reward or punishment for the other side's behaviour. Thus, it is good to see the normal processes of naval togetherness between China and the US continuing despite their recent frictions over the South China Sea. Clearly, making such negotiated arrangements work in practice is critical too. Unless there is actually some responsible person on the other end of a hotline set up after much debate, such arrangements are likely to do more harm than good.

More broadly, exactly the same might be said about the recent meeting of Presidents Xi and Park with Mr Abe.[6] Such an exchange does not mean that the islands of the East China Sea or the historic antipathies that divide these countries have gone away, merely that they do not preclude and indeed may well be mitigated by routine and generally reassuring exchanges. The Joint Declaration for Peace and Cooperation in Northeast Asia, for example, that followed the summit identified the three leaders' desire to work towards greater economic integration as a way of defusing otherwise fraught relationships.

One problem they all face in this kind of diplomatic engagement is the problem of the nationalistic netizen. Whatever their political colour, governments around the world are getting increasingly sensitive to the influence of the social media. For reasons which defy the logic of the Manchester School, xenophobic and strongly nationalist groups seem to be emerging in many countries of the region. For them, the security of the island possessions, say, is increasingly being seen as a performance indicator of the effectiveness – even the legitimacy – of their governments. At a time when governments everywhere are struggling to provide essential and affordable services to rising populations and expanding middle classes, this is a dangerous development since it could narrow the political establishment's room to manoeuvre and, worse still, encourage politicians to 'play to the gallery' in such disputes as a matter of political expediency, designed perhaps to compensate for failures elsewhere.[7] Clearly, it would be much better if they did not do that and instead engaged seriously in the management, if not resolution, of international problems.

An open debate about the legitimacy, intentions and role of 'outsiders' in local seas (whether it be the US and India in the East and South China Seas or China in the Indian Ocean) could well usefully shine a torch in dark places. Thus, India is generally concerned about China's growing naval presence in the Indian Ocean area and alarmed about the surprise appearance of a PLA Navy SSN in a Chinese-operated section of a Sri Lankan port and has specifically warned: "What we are beginning to see is the unfolding of China's desire to be a maritime power…If a submarine docks in a port where a submarine has never docked before from that country, it cannot be a development without repercussions".[8] In a similar vein, the announcement in

November 2016 that China intends to create a 'naval base' in Djibouti reawakened fears that China was indeed in the process of setting up its much-discussed 'string of pearls' across the Indian Ocean in defence of its general trading interests in and across the area. Given that for years China has roundly condemned the establishment of such foreign bases as inherently aggressive, this reversal of view has, rightly or wrongly, caused some alarm in New Delhi and elsewhere.[9]

Closely linked to this is the issue of transparency and clarity, which together tends to reduce the misperceptions and miscalculations that historically have so bedevilled the international relations of the past. This is particularly important in an age of instantaneous and all too often inaccurate news coverage. The Subi Reef affair is an example of a problem aggravated by confusing, and maybe confused, political messaging. There is a tactical case for studied ambiguity since it preserves options for an uncertain future and avoids the necessity for choice from among the policy positions of the various internal stakeholders. But, the strategic dangers of this in the age of the social media and the all too common construction of dangerously misleading national 'narratives' are clearly considerable and make the management and resolution of local problems more difficult.

The same is true of naval planners whose problem in having to peer—as they always have to—'through a glass darkly'. The more obscure one country's naval preparations, the more likely are its neighbours and rivals to overcompensate in their responses. Accordingly, as much transparency as the situation allows, should surely be the norm. This kind of tactical engagement can be implemented through a variety of means, though the production of publicly available doctrines, staff college exchanges, multinational naval exercises, credible and meaningful naval policy papers and so forth. It is often remarked that because they all confront the common dangers of a sometimes hostile sea, there is a natural fraternity amongst sailors. Since to know is often to understand, the more they interact, the better the state of international relations. Moreover, the greater the habits of cooperation, the more effectively can they respond in common to urgent events like catastrophes and other such threats to the international system, that are clearly beyond the power of individual nations to resolve.

Maritime Engagement: The Institutional Angle

Finally, there is the institutional dimension to maritime engagement. Sates can seek to advance the cooperative cause by engaging positively with as many partners and in as many sea-related institutions as their resources and interests allow. Such a policy has its critics, however. Realists looking at ASEAN and the family of institutions it has set up complain of many of these being little more than talking shops which have "little real impact on the region's strategic challenges, such as major shifts in the balance of power, skewed distributions of economic weight, political and cultural homogeneity, territorial disputes and anaemic security institutionalism". Asia reportedly has at least 100 Track 1 channels for security dialogue and more than 200 Track 2 unofficial equivalents.[10] Even so, it has failed to operationalise the 2002 Declaration of Conduct on the South China Sea and ASEAN's failings over the response to Hurricane Haiyan in the Philippines or the search for MH 370, all of which have been much commented upon. This would seem to lend strength to the view that institutions are only as effective as their members wish them to be and are better seen as a consequence of stability and improving relationships than as a cause for them.

A multilateral policy of 'multi-alignment' then may look as though it produces nothing more than an alphabet soup of competing and autarchic institutions, but nonetheless, getting as widely and as diversely engaged as possible has several advantages for constructive engagement. First, this diversity usefully observes the reality that the Indo-Pacific region is far more diverse than, say, Western and Central Europe in its 'command multilateralism'. Second, even in Europe, many established nations with centuries of interactions behind them and a recent history where they were in concert against what they considered a common threat—the former Soviet Union—have found it necessary to set up an alternate system and institutions to cope with alternate challenges. Thus, when responding to the Paris attacks of November 2015, France decided to invoke Article 42-7 of the European Union's Lisbon Treaty rather than Article 5 of the NATO treaty. It did this, believing that 42-7 allowed it to seek a more flexible, tailored and specific response from its alliance partners. For its part, NATO also has been adjusting itself to face a more complex future and has shown surprising institutional resilience over the years, and is now in the process of setting up forces more capable of rapid responses to unexpected situations.[11] Hence, the value of the complementary NATO and EU approaches to the piracy problem off Somalia.

Third, a plurality of sea-related institutions allows for the breadth of issues that are now being embraced within the apparently limitless concept of maritime security to be dealt with more effectively. These issues include the maintenance of maritime domain awareness, dealing with piracy and other forms of maritime crime, environmental issues, search and rescue, humanitarian relief operations, incident and crisis management processes and so on. It is generally encouraging to see the extent to which multilateral institutions designed to encourage discourse on maritime matters steadily growing in number and ambition. An interesting recent development was the decision of the East Asia Summit of November 2015 to enhance the importance of the East Asia Maritime Forum.[12]

Fourth, institutional diversity provides a means by which smaller and weaker states can preserve their interests in a world otherwise dominated by the great and powerful. Nor does this approach necessarily compete with the current fashion of setting up regional security partnerships of one sort or another as a means by which smaller nations can guard against the danger of being given 'a good ignoring'.

Fifth and finally, as Churchill once said that for all its faults, "jaw, jaw is better than war, war." One of the key differences between the situation now when compared to that before the First and Second World Wars—which were likewise periods of economic strain in which the international order was changing with some countries rising and others falling—is that today's processes take place within a constellation of debate and discourse about maritime cooperation. This kind of constructive maritime engagement, in other words, has its undoubted limitations but is still infinitely preferable to the alternative and for that reason alone the setting up of this International Fleet Review deserves to be warmly welcomed, not least as it contributes to a schedule of varied exercises in naval togetherness that increasingly seems continuous and routine—just, of course, as they should.

Notes

1. Mazarr, Michael. "Rivalry's New Face", *Survival,* Vol 54 No 4, Aug-Sep 2012, pp. 83-106.
2. There are exceptions of course, since economic rationality is not the only driver of human behaviour.
3. Xiaoming Liu, China's Ambassador to London. "Take the New Silk Road as an Opportunity not a Threat", *Financial Times,* 24 May 2015, http://www.ft.com/intl/cms/s/0/c8f58a7c-ffd6-11e4-bc30-00144feabdc0.html#axzz44BjxOvn5.
4. Quoted in Cigui, Liu. "Reflections on Maritime Partnership: Building the 21st Century Maritime Silk Road". Beijing: China Institute of International Studies, 15 Sep 2014, http://www.ciis.org.cn/english/2014-09/15/content_7231376.htm .
5. Wade, Geoff. "The Pre-Modern East Asian Maritime Realm" in in Satish Chandra and Himanshu Prabha Ray (eds), *The Sea, Identity and History: From the Bay of Bengal to the South China Sea.* Singapore: ISEAS, 2013, p. 102.
6. Choon, Chang My. "China, S. Korea, Japan Take Big Step to Normalise Ties", *The Straits Times,* 2 Nov 2015, http://www.straitstimes.com/asia/china-s-korea-japan-take-big-step-to-normalise-ties, and also; "Trilateral Summit a Promising Step", *The*

Straits Times, 7 Nov 2015, http://www.straitstimes.com/opinion/trilateral-summit-a-promising-step.

7. Zongqiang, Jiang and Hu Xin. "China's Dilemma: Populists could Hijack Policy Response", *The Straits Times,* 3 Dec 2015,
8. A senior Indian Foreign Ministry official quoted in Niharika Mandhana, "Modi Heads to China as Asian Alliances Shift", *Wall Street Journal*, 15 May 2015, http://www.pressreader.com/china/the-wall-street-journal-asia/20150513
9. Yung, Christopher D. '"Not an Idea We have to Shun: Chinese Overseas basing Requirements in the 21st Century". Washington; NDU, INSS Perspective 7, October 2014.
10. Choong, William. *The Ties That Divide*. London: Routledge for the IISS, 2014, p. 120.
11. Barnes, Julian E. "NATO Security Role Faces Reassessment", *Wall Street Journal,* 20 Nov 2015, http://www.pressreader.com/china/the-wall-street-journal-asia/20151126/281543699837139/TextView.
12. Available at http://www.asean.org/images/2015/November/10th-EAS-Outcome/EAS%20Statement%20on%20Enhancing%20Regional%20Maritime%20Cooperation%20-%20FINAL%2022%20November%202015.pdf.

10. The Indonesian Approach and Perspective on Asia's Regional Maritime Cooperative Engagements

Amarulla Octavian

Introduction

The twenty-first century has marked the rise of Asia. The region is now the centre of gravity of global politics, economy and security due to its significant and robust economic development and growth. The region's economic drivers rely heavily on sea routes to ship their goods and energy, particularly along the Pacific and Indian Oceans. Hence, the discussions on the rise of Asia would eventually include these two oceans.

In terms of regional security, it is interesting to note that 40 per cent of the global territorial disputes are located in the Asian region. According to a research, one-third of Asia's ongoing disputes are over offshore islands. The South China Sea dispute is one of the most prominent territorial disputes in the region. Asia also has the highest concentration of nuclear weapons in the world.[1] Competition and conflict are quite high in the region; particularly in the maritime domain, since countries in the region are enhancing and upgrading their naval forces. However, the region is also seeing many forms of security arrangements which some see as capable of maintaining peace and security, while others believe that more should be done.

The rise of Asia has also returned the Indian Ocean into the spotlight. It provides crucial shipping and trade routes connecting the Middle East, Africa and South Asia with other Asian and European countries as well. Around half of the global crude oil demand is shipped daily through some of the IOR's strategic choke points.

Further, social interactions, of both regional and extra-regional kind, have intensified among the nations. Some of these are quite old and some relatively new. These nation-based social interactions have created competition, conflicts as well as cooperation in the process, thereby influencing the geostrategic and the security environment of the Asian region.

As an archipelagic state connecting the Pacific Ocean and the Indian Ocean, Indonesia understands the significance of the maritime domain along with its safety and security. Indonesia is actively engaged in the regional maritime cooperative arrangements, particularly the Indonesian Navy. Hence, it could offer its experiences in existing cooperative frameworks, as well as its perspective and approaches for future arrangements. This chapter focusses on the current strategic environment of Asia, in particular the Indian Ocean Region (IOR) and the Western Pacific, which will include the existing competition and conflict. It also looks at the existing cooperation in both these regions and provides Indonesia's experience, approach and perspective on future cooperative arrangements, which will include the importance of the use of the arbitration framework as a resolution mechanism and the need for a 'new law of the sea' mechanism.

Asia and Its Current Strategic Environment

Asia is a diverse and complex region. It has gone through a number of major transitions[2] since the end of World War II, including the transformation from being poor countries torn by World Wars and regional conflicts into the world's economic centre of graviιy it has also experienced a major regional shift due to the rise of China.[3] Therefore, even though diverse, experts have identified a number of 'contemporary characteristics' of the Asian region, which are: (a) state-centrism with embedded norms favouring state sovereignty; (b) a distinctive form of economic integration along with a growing economic asymmetry; (c) dual forms of strategic uncertainty, where all countries are facing difficulties in adjusting to an increasingly Sino-centric region and world; (d) a growing economic capacity for military modernisation with possible security dilemmas; (e) a porous region; (f) a proliferation of informal organisational frameworks, particularly of an economic character, and (g) a reduced intensity of ideological divisions post-Cold War.[4]

This region has indeed transformed significantly. In a 2011 report titled *Asian 2050: Realizing the Asian Century*, the Asian Development Bank (ADB) had forecast from an economic perspective that Asia's 2050 per capita income may increase up to six times[5] led by the drivers of Asia's economic engine—namely, China, India, Indonesia, Japan, Republic of Korea, Thailand and Malaysia.[6] In 2010, these seven countries had a combined population of 3.1 billion, which is 78 per cent of the total population of Asia, and a total GDP of US$ 15.1 trillion or 87 per cent of Asia's GDP.[7] The same ADB report forecasted that in 2050 these countries' combined population would cover 75 per cent of Asia's population and

90 per cent of the region's GDP. On a global scale, these Asian economic drivers could reach 53 per cent of the world's GDP between 2010 and 2050, making them "the engines of not only Asia's economy but also the global economy."[8]

Rapid and robust economic growth in Asia has allowed the regional countries to improve their military power, particularly navy-related armaments. Asian defence spending has increased significantly by around 27 per cent between 2010 and 2014, mostly on naval and air force procurements.[9] In 2012, Asia defeated the defence budget of NATO's members from the European continent.[10] At a time when global military spending continues to fall since 2012, Asia's (and Oceania) continues to rise; reaching 5 per cent in 2014 and being worth US$ 439 billion.[11]

One of the reasons for such a spike in military spending is the South China Sea dispute. It has been discussed by analysts since the 1990s that it could push the countries in the region—both the claimant and non-claimant states— to increase their military power, particularly their navies.[12] These countries are anxious about China's rapid island-building[13] and logistics and military facilities in the disputed waters as well as its practices of assertive action with other claimants at sea.[14]

Another maritime boundary dispute in the region that has occupied much of the international community's interest is the East China Sea. Unlike the South China Sea dispute, the East China Sea maritime boundary dispute has only two claimant states: China and Japan. Both countries are in dispute over the Senkaku (Japan) or Diaoyu (China) Islands that lie in the East China Sea. Even though the implications of this dispute may not be as grand as the other, the tension between the two countries has encouraged Japan to increase its defence spending and allowing its defence forces to have more power in facing China's activities in the disputed waters. In December 2015, Japan announced its record-high defence budget for the fiscal year 2016/2017: over 5 trillion yen or around US$ 41.4 billion.[15] There are claims that the defence budget will focus much on strengthening Japan's position in the Senkaku/Diaoyu Islands through the procurement of amphibious warfare capabilities.[16]

These maritime disputes do not involve only those who are party to the claims. The United States, with its interest in freedom of navigation and overflight in both seas, as well as having two of its close allies in the region—Japan and Philippines—as claimants to these disputes, also plays an important role in the dynamics of these disputes which in the Western Pacific reflect the rivalry between China, the rising power, and the United States. The former seems eager to push away the latter's hegemony in the region. These are the outstanding competitions and conflicts in the Western Pacific.

The Indian Ocean has its own complex narrative. As the world's third largest ocean, the Indian Ocean has six key characteristics:[17] (a) it is a semi-enclosed ocean; (b) it has abundant energy resources, minerals and commodities; (c) it is at the global centre of geostrategic and economy, integrated with the Western Pacific; (d) interstate competition and many territorial or maritime conflicts exist herein; (e) it is one of the world's main SLOCs for energy transportation, and (f) it is part of the rise of maritime Asia. Its ports manage around 30 per cent of the global trade and 50 per cent of the overall global container traffic.[18]

Transportation of energy through the seas is one of the reasons why the Indian Ocean region is becoming increasingly important to the international community. Around 32.2 millions of barrels of crude oil and petroleum are shipped daily through some of IOR's strategic chokepoints, such as the Straits of Hormuz and Malacca.[19] It is forecast that by 2025, the demand for oil would reach 118 million barrels per day (bpd), from 82.5 million bpd in 2004.[20] Almost 80 per cent of India's energy resources are imported, while in 2012 alone, 84 per cent of China's energy resources were being transported through the Malacca Strait from the Indian Ocean.[21]

The region is also considered home to some of the world's protracted conflicts and a majority of failed/fragile states. A report by the Heidelberg Institute for International Conflict Research found that 42 per cent of the global conflict could be associated with the countries in the IOR[22] and *Foreign Policy's* 2009 'Failed State Index' included 11 IOR states in its list of 20 failed and failing states.[23] These politically unstable countries have driven activities such as piracy, human and drug trafficking as well as maritime terrorism among other maritime security threats in the region including environmental issues, maritime boundary disputes, Humanitarian Assistance Disaster Relief (HA/DR) and Search and Rescue (SAR). HA/DR issues are important for the IOR, in particular after the 2004 tsunami. As can be seen in Figure 1, natural disasters are a major contributor to the region's challenges and threats.

One crucial maritime security issue in the Indian Ocean in the past decade has been of piracy in the Horn of Africa, where Somali pirates terrorised the shipping and seafaring community by hijacking and demanding ransom in exchange of the crews taken hostage. A 2014 report on NATO's Operation Ocean Shield recorded a significant decrease in pirate activities in the Gulf of Aden from 45 hijacks, 130 attacks and 62 disruptions in 2009 to zero hijacks, a single attack and zero disruption in 2014.[24] The International Maritime Bureau (IMB) reported 75 incidents in the Gulf of Aden and the Red Sea in 2012, while in August 2014, only 10 major cases were reported, which included two hijackings.[25] Some experts claim these reports signify a substantial decrease in piracy and hijacking cases in the area, largely because of the efforts of multilateral navies.[26] The issue of Somali piracy, however, could still worsen due to a lack of security and stability where piracy provides better economic rewards to the people of Somalia.

If the Western Pacific is the arena for Sino-America rivalry, the Indian Ocean Region is the theatre where two of Asia's rising powers, China and India, compete with one another for influence and resources. In terms of military spending, both countries have increased their budget by double digits in 2015 as can be seen in Figure 1, with no signs of a slowdown in the near future. China will establish its first naval base in Djibouti,[27] while India just released its new maritime strategy titled "Ensuring Secure Seas: Indian Maritime Security Strategy" late last year.[28] Their competition does not stop at flexing military muscle. China and India have formulated and developed their initiatives[29] in the region as well as forged ties with other countries in the IOR, particularly smaller ones, in order to ensure their security and economic interests.[30]

Figure 1. Indian Ocean by the Numbers

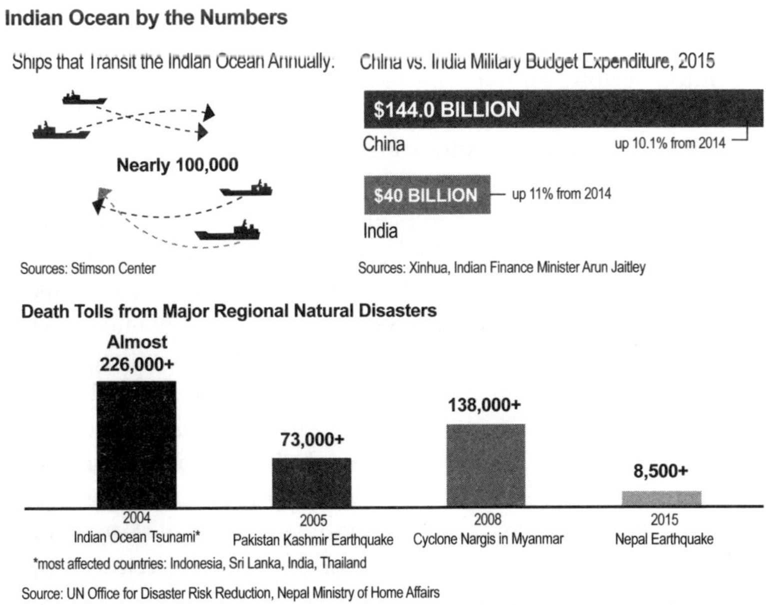

Source: Council for Foreign Research (CFR) Backgrounder, *Competition in the Indian Ocean*, November 2015

Competition, Conflict and Cooperation

Humans are social beings who undergo social interactions and processes on a regular or daily basis, from the individual level till the state or even regional ones. Among the many possible social interactions that may occur at the state level, we could identify conflict, competition and cooperation as the ones that happen most often. In fact, they are the engines of our international community. Countries compete, cooperate and dispute with each other.

A.W. Green defines conflict as "the deliberate attempt to oppose, resist or coerce the will of another or others"[31] while Gillin and Gillin describe it as "the social process in which individuals or groups seek their ends by directly challenging the antagonist by violence or threat of violence."[32] Green then defines cooperation as "the continuous and common endeavour of two or more persons to perform a task or to reach a goal that is commonly cherished" while Merrill and Eldredge explain cooperation as "a form of social interaction wherein two or more persons work together to gain a common end". Charles Cooley believes that both conflict and cooperation are inseparable; they are phases of a single process. No matter how close two individuals, groups or states are, when particular interests come into play, the possibility of conflict may rise in the midst of robust cooperation.

Competition, on the other hand, is defined by Sutherland, Woodword and Maxwell as an "impersonal, unconscious, continuous struggle between individuals and groups for satisfaction which, because of their limited supply, all may not have". Biesanz and Biesanz state that competition "is the striving of two or more persons for the same goal which is limited so that all cannot share it". Forms of competition can be economic, cultural, social, racial and political.

These sociological theories remain relevant for today's international relations. On the international level, a state's relation to another, either bilateral or multilateral, could be in the form of dissociative or associative interaction. The first destroys social ties, tends to estrange one or the other or is negative by nature, and includes competition and conflict. The latter, on the other hand, strengthens social ties, brings one party closer to the other or is positive, implemented through various kinds of cooperation.

As explained earlier, Asia has its fair share of competitions, conflicts and even cooperation. The East and South China Seas disputes clearly reflect both competition and conflict among the claimant states and could even involve non-claimant or extra-regional states. The IOR has become an arena for Sino-Indian rivalry.

Before moving on to cooperation in Asia, it is important to note the role of territorial disputes, including the maritime ones, in the relations among states in the region and beyond. Some researchers[33] have found a distinctive connection between a territorial dispute between two countries and the possibility of such dispute being militarised.[34] This connection is very important for Asia since in 2000 it was home to almost 40 per cent of the world's active territorial disputes, and between 1945 until 2000, the region has accounted for 28 per cent of such disputes in the world.[35] It is also the region where 34 per cent of the global territorial disputes have been militarised.[36] A third of the territorial disputes in Asia are over offshore islands, and only one-third of those maritime disputes have been settled.[37]

Some studies, nevertheless, show the connection between economic resources and territorial dispute settlements, particularly maritime ones.[38] Today's global economy is interconnected, and so regional countries have common interest in the issues of freedom of navigation and secure SLOCs. Hence, states are likely to take measures to avoid any further conflict at sea.

An example of an economic consideration and cooperation between disputed states is the Ems-Dollart Treaty between Germany and the Netherlands. The dispute, which goes back to the fifteenth century, is about the two countries' maritime demarcation in the North Sea. A previous Ems-Dollart Treaty of 1960 did provide regulations for the maritime demarcation between zero and three nautical miles from the coastal line.[39] Nevertheless, it did not regulate the waters between three and 12 nautical miles from the coast. The tension escalated after an offshore wind farm was constructed in the disputed area.[40]

A breakthrough was attained during the political talks between the two countries since 2011, in which a political compromise was achieved at Delfzijl, Holland, in August 2013 called "Agreed Cornerstones."[41] It provided four guiding principles for Germany and the Netherlands to formulate a legally binding bilateral agreement which committed both sides to: (a) maintain their legal standpoint concerning the course of the border; (b) commitment to the principle of good cooperation; (c) competences and responsibilities regarding non-living natural resources split up by an administrative line and (d) the establishment of a joint maritime traffic management system.[42]

The treaty was signed by the two countries on 24 October 2014 which regulates the responsibilities and rights of use for the coastal sea between three and 12 nautical miles from the coast. This legally binding bilateral agreement is special for two specific reasons. First, since the most disagreeable point was discussed openly by the two countries and practical questions had been well addressed, the border issue had little importance; second, Germany and the Netherlands opted for a non-traditional approach through shared responsibilities and a joint decision-making process.[43]

Asia's Existing Regional Maritime Cooperative Frameworks

Since maritime affairs are dominant in the Asian region, maritime-related cooperation or multilateralism is an important tool for regional states, especially for those practicing sea power in exerting and ensuring their national interest in the region.[44] There are multiple organisations for advancing regional cooperation in the Asian region, both among the states in the Western Pacific and those in the Indian Ocean. Most of the issues for cooperation are related to the maritime dimension.

In the Asia-Pacific, there is the Association of Southeast Asian Nations or ASEAN.[45] It is the "driver's seat" in a number of ASEAN-related and expanded multilateral establishments, such as the ASEAN Regional Forum (ARF),[46] a discussion forum for regional foreign ministers as well as the East Asia Summit (EAS)[47] with members from the Asian countries as well as extra-regional states, such as the United States and Russia. In the security domain, ASEAN has developed a special forum for its defence ministers, the ASEAN Defence Ministers' Meeting (ADMM), which was immediately expanded to ADMM-Plus and focuses on five priority areas of maritime security, counter-terrorism, disaster management, peacekeeping operations and military medicine.

ADMM is not the only forum ASEAN expanded to include its extra-regional partners; the ASEAN Maritime Forum (AMF) was also expanded to include the member states of EAS and was subsequently named the Expanded ASEAN Maritime Forum (EAMF) to accommodate further discussions among the ASEAN member countries on maritime-related issues.

In terms of navy-related fora, there is the Western Pacific Naval Symposium (WPNS), initiated by the US Navy. The biennial forum allows the Western Pacific Chief of the Navies to sit together and discuss the regional maritime security issue in an open and friendly manner. At the naval operational level, there is the Malacca Strait Patrols (MSP) by the navies of Indonesia, Malaysia, Singapore and Thailand, and will be discuss further in this paper.

The case is a bit different for the IOR and some perceive the Indian Ocean as lacking "region-wide security architecture, a common regional identity, a history of regional cooperation, or accepted regional leadership frameworks".[48] Geographical constraints and minimum interest among IOR states has contributed to this lack of multilateral structures.[49]

This does not mean that the region has no existing regional framework. There is the voluntary Indian Ocean Naval Symposium (IONS). Initiated by the Indian Navy in 2008, this forum is similar to the WPNS. It, however, does not include extra-regional navies that have a substantial presence in the IOR.[50] Next is the Contact Group on Piracy off the Coast of Somalia (CGPCS), established on 14 January 2009 for information-sharing among state and non-state actors (organisations and industry groups) interested in combating piracy in the Gulf of Aden.[51] The Indian Ocean Rim Association (IORA) has also included maritime security issues as one of the topics in its discussions. Nevertheless, the IOR still necessitates a multilateral framework that includes extra-regional states or navies for managing the region's current and ongoing maritime security issues.

Indonesia's Experiences

As brought out earlier, Indonesia lies in between the Indian and Pacific Oceans, right in the heart of Asia. It is also member of almost every multilateral framework stated previously. Based on its experiences, Indonesia could share its approach and perspectives on Asia's maritime cooperative arrangements.

MSP and WFQR

When the international community highlighted the safety and security of the Malacca Straits, the navies of Indonesia, Malaysia and Singapore launched the Malaysia-Singapore-Indonesia (Malsindo) Trilateral Coordinated Patrol on 20 July 2004. It was then followed by the launch of Eyes-in-the-Sky (EiS) in September 2005.[52] Proposed by Malaysia, EiS supports the coordinated patrol by surface warships of the three navies. Malacca Strait Patrols (MSP) was formed after it was formulated by the MSP Joint Coordinating Committee (JCC) along with its Terms of Reference (TsOR) and the Standard Operating Procedure (SOP).

In its beginning, the MSP consisted of the Malsindo Coordinated Patrol, which transformed into the Malacca Strait Patrol (MSSP) in April 2006, and EiS. MSP itself is a cooperative exercise focusing on close coordination among the littoral countries along the Malacca Strait—Indonesia, Malaysia, Singapore and Thailand— to handle and counter the maritime security issues in the Straits of Malacca and Singapore.

The Intelligence Exchange Group (IEG) was then formed in order to support the MSP and EiS by providing intelligence data for the air and sea coordinated patrols through the MSP Information System (MSP-IS).[53] It allows the exchange of data and information regarding the coordinated patrols among the four navies.

The Royal Thai Navy (RTN) officially joined the MSP after its Commander-in Chief signed the revised MSP TOR and SOP on 18 September 2008 in Thailand. The fact that Thailand joined MSP reflects the ASEAN spirit and at the same time strengthens the MSP's legality and effectiveness in the face of the International Maritime Organization

(IMO) as well as other maritime-related organisations round the world as well as the maritime community.[54]

Statistics show the result of the four-navy effort since it was first established in 2004. The IMO's Annual Report on Acts of Piracy and Armed Robbery against Ships from 1996 until 2010 shows a significant decrease of cases of piracy in the strait, particularly after the launch of the MSSP in 2004, from 60 incidents in 2004 to zero in 2010.[55] The United Nations has also expressed its appreciation and acknowledgement of the success of the MSP, as was seen in an interview with one of the organisation's officials in 2012 who stated that as a sophisticated system, the MSP could bring down piracy cases in the Malacca Strait to zero in 2011.[56] In practice, naval operations would not only cover the Straits of Malacca and Singapore, but also the Natuna Sea and the Gulf of Thailand.

Nevertheless, the efforts of the four navies through the joint naval operations are not without challenges. As the four navies continue to improve their coordination and interoperability through their patrols, this busy strait has once again come into the headlines among the maritime community. Reports of petrol siphoning[57] in the Malacca Strait and calling the strait "the new sea piracy hot spot"[58] or "the new piracy capital of the world"[59] have become major concerns for the navies of the littoral states.

As one of the navies of the littoral states, the Indonesian Navy has taken this issue very seriously. Its Western Fleet Command established the Western Fleet Quick Response (WFQR)[60] as a concrete reaction to assure the maritime and international community that the Malacca Strait is safe and secure. The WFQR has brought to closure a number of cases that had caught the attention of the regional and international community, including the hijacking of the MT Orkim Harmony,[61] MT Joaquim[62] and robbery on board the MV Merlin.[63] The assistance and cooperation received from the neighbouring countries were also very helpful in closing these criminal cases.[64]

Frameworks for Enhancing Interoperability at Sea

During March–April 2014, the Indonesian Navy hosted its first multilateral naval exercise, codenamed Komodo, which was also the first non-warfighting exercise for the navies of the ASEAN-Plus countries. This exercise focused on disaster relief operations and succeeded in formulating an SOP for the ASEAN-Plus joint naval operations on disaster relief. The first test for this new SOP was the SAR operations for Air Asia flight QZ8510 that crashed in the Java Sea off the coast of Kalimantan on 28 December 2014.

During the 2014 WPNS in Qingdao, China, the Chiefs of Navy agreed upon the Code for Unplanned Encounters at Sea (CUES). This non-legally binding document "offers safety procedures, a basic communications plan and basic manoeuvring instructions for naval ships and naval aircraft during unplanned encounters at sea". Aimed to maximise the safety at sea, some have proposed the naval protocol to be expanded and best utilised by other maritime forces outside the navy such as the coast guards.[65]

Both the Komodo Exercise and the WPNS have provided regional navies the operational-level documents or tools to enhance the interoperability at sea. The next step is to formulate a common doctrine and collective Standard Operating Procedures (SOP) for cooperation at sea, perhaps even with the navies beyond the region.

Arbitration as Part of a Resolution Mechanism

As explained earlier, conflict, competition and cooperation mirror some forms of social interactions. The latter is an associative type of social interaction, while the first two are dissociative. The next associative social interaction relevant here is accommodation, which could be in the form of a process or condition. As a process, accommodation suggests efforts to avoid, decrease or eliminate conflicts or dispute. As a condition, it is a state where relations among the social elements are in harmony and balance so that a society, or as in this matter, a state, could easily adapt itself to the hopes or goals it wishes to achieve.[66]

Accommodation aims to reduce interstate discord as a result of different interests through new agreements seen from respective national interests, which are different. It could also be practised to prevent possible conflict for a certain period of time. This type of social interaction is also practised to allow cooperation between or among the States involved in the disputes and which are separated from each other due to psychological or cultural factors.

There are various forms of accommodation, but in the context of international relations, two come to mind: conciliation and arbitration. The first is an institutional effort that allows the parties involved to sit together and to achieve a common agreement, while the latter is a conflict resolution effort through a third party with the authority to settle the dispute.

Both conciliation and arbitration are some of the dispute settlement mechanisms stated in the United Nations (UN) Charter in Chapter VI on Pacific Settlement of Disputes.[67] They are practised in the world of international business and trade and have become more common in the era of globalisation, particularly in the field of arbitration. There are a number of international courts of arbitration for international commerce, such as the International Chamber of Commerce (ICC), the International Centre of Dispute Resolution (ICDR), the Singapore International Arbitration Centre (SIAC), the London Court of International Arbitration (LCIA), the

International Branch of the American Arbitration Association (AAA) and the International Centre for the Settlement of Investment Disputes (ICSID).

Arbitration is one of the dispute settlement mechanisms incorporated within UNCLOS 1982 in case of countries having a different interpretation and application of the convention's provisions.[68] It includes bringing the case to the International Tribunal for the Law of the Sea (ITLOS),[69] an arbitral tribunal or a special arbitral tribunal.[70] The most recent case involves that of the Philippines made against the Chinese claims in the South China Sea at the Permanent Court of Arbitration or PCA, the Hague, initiated on 22 January 2013.[71]

The application of arbitration as a dispute mechanism in bilateral and multilateral cooperation, especially for maritime security, should be considered. It provides a degree of freedom and equality as well as legal authority to the parties involved.

Maritime disputes are clearly one of Asia's sources of possible conflict in the future. Although no country desires any armed conflict at sea, particularly along important shipping lanes such as the South China Sea, the Malacca Strait or waters along the IOR because it would create havoc and stagnations in global economy and create regional and international instability, there is a need to ensure the existence of international rules and norms to govern such action.

International rules and norms for armed conflict at sea or naval warfare have not evolved in ways similar to those for the armed conflict on land. The most current rules for naval warfare is the San Remo Manual on International Law Applicable to Armed Conflicts at Sea or simply, the San Remo Manual, in 1994.[72] The San Remo Manual has a unique position within the international law. As a manual, it is considered as one of the sources for international law.[73] Many countries have adopted the manual into their respective national laws and for Indonesia, the San Remo Manual is part of its Humanitarian Law in regard to the state defence management.[74]

Hence, an arbitration mechanism as part of a dispute settlement arrangement for a maritime cooperative arrangement could utilise the San Remo Manual as one of its legal bases for resolving the disputes at sea since the manual regulates the obligations and rights of the involved and neutral parties.

Time for a New UNCLOS?

The year 2012 marked the thirtieth anniversary of the UNCLOS 1982 that was signed by 164 parties, including the countries of the European Union.[75] The convention was a true milestone in regard to the international law of the sea as it provided international rules and norms as well as regimes, such as the Exclusive Economic Zone (EEZ). Nevertheless, there are parts that could be interpreted in different ways by different countries, including military activities such as exercises and aircraft overflight around the EEZ area, armed conflict at sea and maritime claims and the dispute mechanisms.

Much has changed since the UNCLOS 1982 was opened for signature on 10 December 1982 from rapid technological advancement, Revolution in Military Affairs (RMA) to the changes in global geopolitics. These changes have had significant implications on how warships operate and manoeuvre or how surveys are conducted at sea.

There have been a number of efforts to formulate some guidelines on the above issues to fill the gaps that remain within the UNCLOS 1982.[76] However, these documents are non-binding and do not have provisions about consequential repercussions if a country violates the guidelines since they are based on voluntary adherence.

On the other hand, there is an urgent need for a binding international law that would become the main reference in managing: (a) maritime boundary governance; (b) air space over the sea; (c) securing marine environment and resources; (d) maritime territorial claims and dispute settlement mechanisms; (e) conflicts at sea and means to reduce them; and (f) armed conflict at sea and its resolutions.

Hence, Indonesia believes there is a need to create a new UNCLOS to include the areas that have not been covered in requisite detail under the articles of the Convention in order to reduce possible conflict due to different interpretations and lack of international rules and norms.

Conclusion

The rise of Asia as the world's economic, political and security centre of gravity has its benefits and challenges. Since the seas and oceans are imperative to regional and global economy and security, the issues at sea become increasingly relevant; particularly, the territorial disputes at sea.

Cooperation is the key to ensure regional and global security and stability, and Asia has a number of important and effective cooperative mechanisms. Nevertheless, there are areas which need improvement as well as innovation to answer the challenges of today's dynamic strategic environment and to anticipate the future ones.

As a country that lies at the heart of Asia, between the Indian and Pacific Oceans, Indonesia is actively involved in many of the regions' cooperation mechanisms and has its own approaches and perspectives based on its experiences. There are areas which could be improved, including the use of arbitration and the San Remo Manual in resolution mechanisms as well as formulating a new UNCLOS to anticipate the current trends and development in the maritime domain.

Indonesia believes that developing regional resilience is crucial for facing current and future challenges, particularly in a region that has significant maritime disputes and is an arena of major power rivalries. This resilience should be based on the sincerity of nations to prioritise the regional maritime security and stability.

Notes

1. Pekkanen, Saadia M., John Ravenhill and Rosemary Foot. "The International Relations of Asia" in Pekkanen, Saadia M., John Ravenhill and Rosemary Foot (ed.). *The Oxford Handbook of the International Relations of Asia*, Oxford University Press, 2014, p. 11.
2. Two other major transitions are the process of decolonisation and the move from a theatre for the Cold War into a peaceful region still shadowed by security issues, including territorial disputes, historical legacy and military tensions.
3. Pekkanen, "The International Relations of Asia", Note 1, p. 4.
4. Ibid., p. 5-9 and 15-16.
5. See *Asian 2050: Realizing the Asian Century* Executive Summary p. 3, retrieved from http://adb.org/sites/default/files/asia2050-executive-summary.pdf
6. Ibid., p. 5.
7. Ibid.
8. Ibid.
9. *Military Balance 2015*, the International Institute for Strategic Studies, p. 7
10. Hayton, Bill. *The South China Sea: The Struggle for Power in Asia.* New Haven: Yale University Press, 2014, p. 234.
11. SIPRI. "US Military Spending Falls, Increases in Eastern Europe, Middle East, Africa and Asia Says SIPRI", 13 April 2015, available at http://www.sipri.org/media/pressreleases/2015/milex-april-2015
12. See Schofield, Clive. *An Arms Race in the South China Sea?*, IBRU Boundary and Security Bulletin July 1994, downloadable from https://www.dur.ac.uk/resources/ibru/publications/full/bsb2-2_schofield.pdf.
13. China is not the only one nor is it the first to pursue construction and reclamation activities on the islands and reefs of the South China Sea. However, the scale of its island development is staggering. For example, Malaysia has taken on reclamation at Swallow Reef since the 1980s and expanded the reef from 25 to 85 acres plus an airstrip, a resort and a small naval base, while Vietnam is said to add around 65,000 square metres to West Reef and 21,000 square metres to Sand Cay. China, on the other hand, expanded the Fiery Cross Reef to more than 9,00,000 square metres, including an airstrip, not to mention other reefs in the Spratly and Paracel Islands. For more information, graphics and satellite imageries of these island buildings, see http://amti.csis.org/island-tracker/
14. China employs its "salami-slicing" and "cabbage" strategies to other claimant states. A report for the US Congress explains the first is "a series of incremental actions, none of which by itself is a casus belli, to gradually change the status quo in China's favor", while the latter is a strategy of "consolidating control over disputed islands by wrapping those islands, like the leaves of a cabbage, in successive layers of occupation and protection formed by fishing boats, Chinese Coast Guard ships, and then finally

Chinese naval ships". The report can be downloaded at https://www.fas.org/sgp/crs/row/R42784.pdf

15. http://www.reuters.com/article/us-japan-defence-budget-idUSKBN0U704N20151224
16. Gady, Franz-Stefan. "Japan Approves Defense Budget", 23 December 2015, published online at http://thediplomat.com/2015/12/japan-approves-record-defense-budget/
17. Mohan, Malik. "The Indo-Pacific Maritime Domain: Challenges and Opportunities" in Mohan, Malik (ed.), *Maritime Security in the Indo-Pacific: Perspectives from China, India and the United States*. London: Rowman & Littlefield, 2014, p. 2-5.
18. Potgieter, Thean. "Maritime Security in the Indian Ocean: Strategic Setting and Features", Institute for Security Studies Paper, August 2012, No. 236, p. 2.
19 Albert, Eleanor. "Competition in the Indian Ocean", CFR Backgrounders, 23 November 2015, retrieved from http://www.cfr.org/regional-security/competition-indian-ocean/p37201
20. Mohan, Note 17, p. 5.
21. Albert, Note 19.
22. Potgieter, Note 18.
23. Cordner, Lee. "Progressing Maritime Security Cooperation in the Indian Ocean", *US Naval War College Review*, Autumn 2011, Vol. 64, No.4, p. 74.
24. See http://www.nato.int/nato_static_fl2014/assets/pdf/pdf_topics/141202a-Factsheet-OceanShield-en.pdf
25. Cordesman. Anthony H. and Abdullah Toukan, *The Indian Ocean Region: A Strategic Net Assessment*, Centre for Strategic and International Studies (CSIS), August 2014, p. 187
26. Ibid., p. 188.
27. See http://www.defensenews.com/story/defense/international/mideast-africa/2015/12/04/china-navy-base-djibouti/76786990/
28. Baruah, Darshana M. "India's Evolving Maritime Strategy", 3 December 2015, published online at http://thediplomat.com/2015/12/indias-evolving-maritime-strategy/
29. For example, China's "One Belt One Road (OBOR) initiative and India's Indian Ocean Naval Symposium (IONS).
30. Albert, Note 19.
31. Sharma, Rajendra Kumar. *Social Change and Social Control*, New Delhi: Atlantic Publishers & Dist, 1997, p. 166.
32. Ibid.
33. See Vasquez, John A., and Marie T. Henehan. "Territorial Disputes and the Probability of War, 1816-1992", *Journal of Peace Research*, 2001, 38, 2: p. 123-138.
34. Fravel, M. Taylor. "Territorial and Maritime Boundary Disputes in Asia" in Pekkanen, Saadia M., John Ravenhill and Rosemary Foot (ed.), *The Oxford Handbook of the International Relations of Asia*, Oxford University Press, 2014. p. 525.
35. Ibid., p. 527.
36. Ibid., p. 529.
37. Ibid., p. 543.
38. Ibid. The study was conducted by Paul Huth in 1996 on the subject of territorial dispute. See Huth, Paul K. 1996. "Enduring Rivalries and Territorial Disputes, 1950-1990",

Conflict Management and Peace Science, 15, 1: p. 7-41; See also, Huth, Paul K. *Standing Your Ground: Territorial Disputes and International Conflict.* Ann Arbor: University of Michigan Press, 1996. His other studies on the same subject include Huth, Paul K. "Territory: Why Are Territorial Disputes a Central Cause of International Conflict" in Vasquez, John (ed.), *What do We Know about War?* Boulder, CO: Rowman and Littlefield, 2000.

39. "Pragmatic, Mutually Beneficial Solutions: Germany and the Netherlands Sign the Ems Dollart Treaty", available at http://www.auswaertiges-amt.de/EN/Aussenpolitik/Laender/Aktuelle_Artikel/Niederlande/141024-EmsDollart.html
40. Ibid.
41. Dr Rainer Lassig in his presentation titled "The New Ems-Dollart-Treaty: Progressive Legal Solutions instead of Zero-Sum Games in the Ems Estuary", presented during the 2nd ASEAN-EU High Level Dialogue on Maritime Security Cooperation: "Developing Inter-Agency Cooperation and Regional Cooperation to Enhance Maritime Security, 5 May 2014, Kuala Lumpur, Malaysia.
42. Ibid.
43 Ibid.
44. Sakhuja, Vijay. 2014. "Multilateral Mechanism in the Indo-Pacific" in Mohan, Malik (ed.), *Maritime Security in the Indo-Pacific: Perspectives from China, India, and the United States*, Rowman & Littlefield, London, p. 222.
45. For more information on ASEAN, see http://www.asean.org/
46. For more information on ARF, see http://aseanregionalforum.asean.org/
47. For more information on EAS and its summits, see http://www.asean.org/asean/external-relations/east-asia-summit-eas
48. Cordner, Note 23, p. 69.
49. Sakhuja, Note 44, p. 226.
50 Van der Putten, Frans-Paul, Thorsten Wetzling and Susanne Kamerling. *Geopolitics and Maritime Security in the Indian Ocean: What Role for the European Union?*, Clingendael Institute Policy Brief, August 2014, p. 6
51. Sakhuja, Note 44, p. 227.
52. See http://www.mindef.gov.sg/imindef/press_room/official_releases/nr/2005/sep/13sep05_nr.html#.VTYzMyGqqko and http://www.mindef.gov.sg/imindef/press_room/official_releases/nr/2008/mar/28mar08_nr/28mar08_fs.html#.VTY0PCGqqko
53. See http://www.mindef.gov.sg/imindef/press_room/official_releases/nr/2008/mar/28mar08_nr/28mar08_fs.html#.VTY0PCGqqko
54. See http://www.seatrade-maritime.com/news/asia/asia-piracy-attacks-fall-in-first-nine-months-of-2013.html
55. Data taken from http://www.navedu.navy.mi.th/stg/databasestory/data/Situation-sea/Maritime-Domain-Awareness/Minilateral%20MDA%20Initiatives_CollinKOH_Enhanced.pdf
56. Inter Press Service News Agency interview of Patricia O'Brien who was the UN Under-Secretary-General for Legal Affairs at the time. See http://www.ipsnews.net/2012/08/qa-u-n-spotlights-pirates-in-the-malacca-strait-at-expo-2012/
57. See http://www.aljazeera.com/indepth/features/2015/04/petrol-pirates-proliferate-southeast-asian-seas-150426115129085.html accessed

58. See http://www.marketwatch.com/story/forget-somalia-this-the-new-sea-piracy-hot-spot-2015-10-07
59. See http://www.economist.com/news/asia/21656237-step-aside-somalia-south-east-asia-new-piracy-capital-world-malacca-buccaneers
60. This mechanism was established on 1 December 2014. It comprises close cooperation and coordination between the Maritime Security Task Force, Western Fleet Command and Indonesian Navy's five Main Naval Bases; Main Naval Base Belawan, Main Naval Base Padang, Main Naval Base Jakarta, Main Naval Base Tanjung Pinang and Main Naval Base Pontianak.
61. For further information on the MT Orkim Harmony case, see http://worldmaritimenews.com/archives/164324/orkim-harmony-hijackers-confess/ and http://www.reuters.com/article/2015/06/19/us-malaysia-missing-tanker-idUSKBN0OZ07020150619
62 For further information on the MT Joaquim case see https://sg.news.yahoo.com/mt-joaquim-found-crew-safe-051932886.html
63. For further information on the MV Merlin case see http://www.melayutoday.com/berita-1538-dalam-waktu-3-hari-koarmabar-tangkap-perompak-di-kawasan-selat-malaka-.html and http://m.news.viva.co.id/news/read/690814-tni-al-tangkap-dua-kawanan-perompak-di-selat-malaka
64. In the MT Orkim Harmony case, the WFQR team cooperated with authorities from Vietnam in tracking the escaped perpetrators. For the MT Joaquim, the WFQR team closely cooperated with the Malaysian Maritime Enforcement Agency (MMEA) and in the MV Merlin robbery case, the WFQR team coordinated closely with the Maritime Singapore Task Force (MSTF). See http://www.melayutoday.com/berita-1538-dalam-waktu-3-hari-koarmabar-tangkap-perompak-di-kawasan-selat-malaka-.html, https://sg.news.yahoo.com/mt-joaquim-found-crew-safe-051932886.html and http://m.news.viva.co.id/news/read/690814-tni-al-tangkap-dua-kawanan-perompak-di-selat-malaka
65. In a regional security forum in early December 2015, the newly-appointed Chief of Royal Malaysian Navy (RMN), Admiral Kamarulzaman Ahmad Badaruddin called for the expansion of CUES to other maritime agencies, in particular the coast guards. Singapore has also expressed a similar idea. These aspirations are influenced by the ongoing tension in the South China Sea. Some experts have also encouraged the use of CUES by civilian maritime agencies, especially by the Chinese Coast Guard in regard to the Sino-US relations. See http://thediplomat.com/2015/12/malaysia-wants-expanded-naval-protocol-amid-south-china-sea-disputes/, http://thediplomat.com/2015/12/singapore-calls-for-more-inclusive-asian-security-order-amid-chinas-rise/ and http://amti.csis.org/china-building-confidence-while-setting-expectations/
66. Gillin and Gillin say "accommodation is the term used by sociologists to describe a process by which competing and conflicting individuals and groups adjust their relationships to each other in order to overcome the difficulties which arise in competition, contravention or conflict".
67. Article 33 of the UN Charter states that "the parties to any dispute, the continuance of which is likely to endanger the maintenance of international peace and security, shall, first of all, seek a solution by negotiation, enquiry, mediation, conciliation, arbitration, judicial settlement, resort to regional agencies or arrangements, or other peaceful

means of their own choice".

68. See United Nations Convention on the Law of the Sea, Part XV on Settlement of Disputes, Article 287.
69. Inaugurated on 18 October 1996.
70 Note 68.
71. For more information on the case see Permanent Court of Arbitration http://www.pcacases.com/web/view/7. The arbitration process is currently ongoing, especially after the arbiters ruled that they do have jurisdiction upon the case as on 29 October 2015. China has expressed its agitation against Philippines's action to take the South China Sea dispute case beyond bilateral efforts and has repeatedly denied the authority of the PCA in ruling such a case. To read more on what may come next after the court's ruling comes out see http://amti.csis.org/possible-consequences-of-the-philippines-south-china-sea-arbitration-case/, http://thediplomat.com/2014/12/why-china-wont-accept-international-arbitration-in-the-south-china-sea/, http://thediplomat.com/2015/07/3-reasons-the-philippines-will-suffer-because-of-its-south-china-sea-case-against-china/ and http://thediplomat.com/2015/08/who-will-win-in-the-philippines-south-china-sea-case-against-china/
72. The Manual's brief history is available at https://www.icrc.org/ihl/INTRO/560?OpenDocument
73. Narwati, Enny. "Aturan Perang di Laut: San Remo Manual sebagai Sumber Hukum Internasional", *Mimbar Hukum*, Volume 20, Number 3, October 2008, p. 451-455, retrieved from https://www.google.co.id/url?sa=t&rct=j&q=&esrc=s&source=web&cd=1&cad=rja&uact=8&ved=0CB8QFjAA&url=http%3A%2F%2Fmimbar.hukum.ugm.ac.id%2Findex.p%2Fjmh%2Farticle%2Fdownload%2F247%2F102&ei=vK6iVYnzLZKfugTMuLPwCg&usg=AFQjCNFskbGz9jnlB9rKYQOSN3ZSJi3iLw&sig2=5MeyJBqr2b1efXfqTVC_lA&bvm=bv.97653015,d.c2E, and Soleh, Mohammad. "Aspek Hukum Internasional mengenai Peperangan di Wilayah Laut Negara Kepulauan", retrieved from http://ejournal.narotama.ac.id/files/SOLEH_PERANG_7.doc
74. See Article 2 and 4 of Minister of Defense of the Republic of Indonesia Regulation Number 9 year 2013 on Implementation of Humanitarian and Human Rights Laws in State Defense Management, available at http://www.djpp.kemenkumham.go.id/arsip/bn/2013/bn324-2013.htm
75 Data as of 24 October 2012. See UNCLOS at 30, p. 2, downloadable from http://www.un.org/depts/los/convention_agreements/pamphlet_unclos_at_30.pdf
76 See "Guidelines for Navigation and Overflight in the Exclusive Economic Zone" published on 16 September 2005 by Ocean Policy Research Foundation, downloadable at https://www.sof.or.jp/en/report/pdf/200509_20051205_e.pdf and "Principles for Building Confidence and Security in the Exclusive Economic Zones of the ASIA-PACIFIC" published on 30 October 2013 by Ocean Policy Research Foundation, downloadable at https://www.sof.or.jp/jp/report/pdf/2014_03_02.pdf

11. Building Partnerships in the Bay of Bengal: Opportunities and Challenges

Ataur Rahman

Introduction

The Bay of Bengal has assumed new significance in recent years in the context of competition for influence among the major maritime powers, especially India, China and the United States, which are focused on the access to energy, trade and sea-lane security. The Bay is located close to the geographical centre of the Indo-Pacific region at the intersection of the expanding zones which are of strategic interest to China and India.[1] The Bay's importance as a geo-economic hub and an integral part of the Indo-Pacific corridor is also accentuated by the growing presence of non-traditional threats in the form of piracy, terrorism, illegal fishing, trafficking, global warming and natural disasters, all of which represent challenges to its maritime security. These challenges are inherently transnational in nature—where dynamics in one part of the system influence events in another, necessitating coordinated security operations by maritime forces and strategic relationships between the stakeholder states.

This chapter examines areas where the littoral states of the Bay can cooperate or where there is a common ground to build partnerships that can be explored. It is assumed that notwithstanding strategic jostling by major powers, creative re-imagining of the geographical advantages, political and cultural linkages and perception of common interests may unlock the potential for regional collaboration as much as in dismantling the artificially constructed boundaries. It is also argued that new forms of collaborative efforts in the maritime domain can be explored. India can initiate a trilateral naval security cooperation with Bangladesh and Myanmar on similar lines like the one that exists between India, Maldives and Sri Lanka.

India conducts joint military exercises with both Bangladesh and Myanmar, which may be expanded into trilateral exercises to address transnational security threats through joint patrols and surveillance in the Bay region. Regional approach and partnerships can have an immensely positive impact on the critical areas of global commons, such as environment, resource management and migration. There is an urgent need to frame a more humane policy for migration that focusses on basic protection for the migrants. While the US has been a 'constant' in terms of delivery of the Common Public Good Service (CPGS) in the region—and it may continue to be the 'lead actor' for some time—it is unlikely to be the 'only' provider of 'net security' in the longer run.[2] A regional approach could be evolved to deal with natural disasters (prevention, mitigation and rehabilitation), fishing, coastal erosion and marine pollution. It is hoped that "a new regionalism" that lies in recognising the Bay's history, as much as its ecology, will transcend the national frontiers.[3] The efforts of multilateral institutions and major and middle powers would, thus, need to be directed towards such 'capacity-building' in the area of public good in the Oceans.

Significance of the Bay

Covering an area of 838,600 square miles in the north-eastern segment of the Indian Ocean, the Bay of Bengal is bordered mostly by India and Sri Lanka to the west, Bangladesh to the north and Myanmar and the Andaman and Nicobar Islands to the east. The principal trade routes for the Persian Gulf to the Strait of Malacca pass south of the Bay. The seven littoral countries that comprise Bangladesh, India, Myanmar, Sri Lanka, Thailand, Malaysia and Indonesia have outlets through this Bay in the north-eastern segment of the Indian Ocean. Because of its deep inland penetration and a facility of communication with the countries of South and Southeast Asia, the Bay is attracting renewed attention catalysed by its strategic links, resource endowments and overall geopolitical significance in a potential yet volatile and unstable region.

In recent times, an emphasis is being given to the bridging of infrastructure and broader connectivity gaps created by rapid development and increase in volume of goods, services, people and capital flows between economies. Indeed, connectivity has become another important variable adding special significance to the Bay that borders some of the world's fastest growing populations and economies. The Bay of Bengal's rim, from South India to Singapore, by way of Myanmar and Malaysia, thus has become pivotal to Asia's economic as well as strategic future.[4]

Resource Endowments

The Bay of Bengal is well-endowed in terms of marine resources as well as oil, natural gas and other minerals. It has a geologic setting similar to that of the Indus River basin and the western margin of the Indian Peninsula.[5] Hydrocarbon resources in the Bay of Bengal are generally located in the deep sea areas. Two important resources in the Bay are oil and natural gas that are located in the seabed sediments of the drainages of the three major river system—the Ganges, the Brahmaputra and the Meghna—over thousands of years. It is being said that as the Bay is rich in resources, it needs scientific exploration. Currently, a number of US (Chevron and Conoco-Phillips), Australia–Singapore (Santos and Kris-Energy), Irish (Tullow) and Indian (ONGC) companies are engaged in exploration and drilling, notably in the offshore regions of the Bay of Bengal. In fact, the Bay region's rising importance is linked also to the evolution of India's offshore petroleum activity. Recent discoveries in both India and Myanmar point to a promising exploration future for the Bay of Bengal. A number of new international E&P companies such as British Gas (BG), British Petroleum (BP), Eni S.p.A. of Italy, Petrobras, Santos and StatoilHydro have gained a foothold on the east coast through farm-in deals and asset swaps with the ONGC.[6]

In addition to energy considerations, currently there is a competition brewing among the littoral states of the Bay as they seek to attain greater shares of the region's fisheries and freshwater resources, particularly fish, which have remained untapped so far. It is the home of myriad species in large quantities, particularly shrimp and tuna, along with some endangered species.[7] Cooperative efforts are needed for preventing unscientific harvesting, thereby destroying this rich protein source. The Bay is a biologically diverse basin and it is considered essential to maintain this unique ecological balance. In this context, it is important to evolve a regional approach or mechanism to address the 'global commons' or resource domains in the Bay that lie outside the political reach of any one State for the economic progress, peace and stability of the entire region. The Bay is also rich in minerals that can be good ingredients for the growth of the littoral states' Blue Economy which is based on the resources of the ocean and for resource-poor countries like Bangladesh, which need to expand their resource base beyond the land and into the sea.

In September 2015, the Indian Ocean Rim Associations hosted the first IORA Ministerial Blue Economy Conference titled "Enhancing Blue Economy Cooperation for Sustainable Development in the IORA Region" in Mauritius and identified four priority areas: (a) Fisheries & Aquaculture; (b) Renewable Ocean Energy; (c) Seaports and Shipping; and (d) Seabed Exploration and Minerals for development. The post-conference declaration urged the member States to engage in the development of the above sectors and strengthen networking, exchange of experiences and best practices for the development of the Blue Economy in the region.[7]

The coastal landmass of the Bay is very fertile due to a regular flush of nutrient-rich silts and supply of organic matters from mangrove litter falls. As a result, it has become one of the richest areas in terms of biological diversity and productivity. However, the Bay of Bengal is probably one of the most understudied areas in the world and there is a lack of comprehensive knowledge about different biological and ecological aspects of the coastal and marine fisheries, which, to some extent, limits the utilisation and management of the resources. Some reports are available describing the different aspects of the Bay of Bengal, but such information is extremely fragmentary and incomplete. It is important to note that the marine environment of the Bay is witnessing an uncontrolled degradation caused by pollution, erosion of coastal strips and oil leakage. It is therefore argued that the environmental security encompassing the common interests of the littoral states of the Bay requires a pooling of State sovereignty in order to protect ecological interests.[8]

Centre of Economic Activities

The Bay of Bengal's importance as a trade route for international commerce is increasing and ambitious ventures are already underway along the eastern half of the Bay. In fact, the harbours on the eastern zone of the Indian Ocean are fast transforming the economic geography of Asia.[9] A large new terminal beside the old harbour in Sittwe (Akyab) as a joint project between India and Myanmar is under development. Taking advantage of the port's site at the mouth of the river Kaladan, which empties into the Bay of Bengal, India hopes to open its own landlocked and impoverished north-eastern states. In Bangladesh, Chittagong is the biggest port in the Bay and its modernisation process includes a new deep-water container terminal. Myanmar is keen for foreign investment to help rebuild its economy and has approved projects that had been kept in abeyance for a long time.[10] The Chinese have built new oil and gas pipelines across Myanmar starting from a new port-terminal at Kyaukphyu, near Sittwe. These pipelines run through Mandalay to Ruili on the border and beyond to Kunming, the capital of the Yunnan province. Sukh Deo Muni of Singapore's Institute of South Asian Studies reckons that the new connectivity will generate more economic activity.[11] At the same time, there are challenges due to a lack of cooperative measures to mitigate disaster, offset the impact of climate change and effectively address interregional migration. With the rise in sea levels and deltaic lands subsiding, saltwater intrusion into the farmlands has accelerated which has serious consequences for food production.

The coastal areas of the Bay are under assault in every dimension—by water conflicts in the Himalayas and by drilling for oil and gas in the deep sea.[12] The resolution of long-standing maritime disputes between Bangladesh and India, and Myanmar and Bangladesh, has inspired new hopes. A talk of blue economy is being predicated on harnessing the resources of the Bay by the littoral states in a cooperative manner. The aforementioned issues make a strong case for evolving a regional approach or mechanism to address the 'global commons' or 'resource domains' in the Bay that lie outside the politico-legal jurisdiction of any one State.

Strategic Environment

Building partnerships among the littoral states of the Bay is a desired goal that can only be achieved when the perceived interests and viewpoints merge into a common vision of freedom, stability and prosperity. The Bay of Bengal has assumed a new significance in recent years as the littoral states maintain convergent as well as differing perceptions in the context of the expanding and competing Chinese and Indian spheres of influence along with those of the US. [13]

Although the focus is on trade and energy security, the key maritime powers are providing assistance to the maritime security forces of the littoral states. Consequently, the Bay region's security context is quickly changing. Three trends are clearly discernible: first, the efforts of the US and to some extent its international partners (India, Australia, Singapore and Japan) to maintain their presence in the Bay and the Indian Ocean in order to achieve key strategic objectives. These include attempts to limit the power and influence of countries such as China, Iran and Russia; secure access to energy sources and engage in counterterrorist operations of varied nature. The second trend is that of China trying to increase its "military and maritime links with countries such as Myanmar, Sri Lanka and Bangladesh" through funding of infrastructure projects and naval presence.[14] The third trend is indicated by the efforts of the Bay states for building their own naval capacity to manage transnational and non-traditional threats including disaster and environmental challenges, fishing infringements, smuggling, trafficking, piracy and security of the offshore installations.

India's Imperatives

A key part of the strategic jostling occurring in the Bay of Bengal involves India's attempts to consolidate its role as a leading maritime power in the Bay. This is perceived by India not only as a means of achieving its economic growth and prosperity but also as its normative responsibility as a regional power. India's recent maritime strategy released in October 2015 indicates its intention to be a provider of 'net security' in its areas of maritime interest, which have been significantly expanded within the Indo-Pacific region, and even beyond. [15]

Such enunciation is in consonance with the Indian Prime Minister's vision of "SAGAR".[16] Furthermore, the role emerges not only from India's normative responsibility as a regional power, but is also closely interwoven with its own economic growth and prosperity. The concept of 'net security' is defined as "...the state of actual security available in an area, upon balancing prevailing threats, inherent risks and rising challenges in the maritime environment, against the ability to monitor, contain and counter all of these".[17] Indeed, the Bay is perceived to be strategically important for India as it provides a considerable strategic leverage against rival powers and tackles the security issues that may directly threaten India's interests, including piracy, smuggling, terrorism and separatist movements. There has been a considerable 'rebalancing' of India's naval resources towards the Bay, reflecting its relatively increased threat perceptions especially in relation to China.

India is also developing extensive military assets in the Andaman and Nicobar Islands, which run north–south through the Andaman Sea, including port facilities and bases for surveillance and strike aircraft.[18] As India's navy has evolved, it has shown an ambition to project power and influence across the IOR and beyond. New Delhi has been building its military power in the Bay region allowing it to potentially dominate the western end of the Malacca Strait and much of the surrounding waters.[19]

China's Expanding Role

China looks at the Bay of Bengal as an important maritime space for its future connectivity, trade and energy links within and across the Indian Ocean security landscape. China's ambition is also propelled by a constellation of strategic, commercial and security considerations. The paramount concern animating the Chinese interests in the Indian Ocean is energy security that is linked with its strategic presence as a maritime power through the building up of a credible naval strength.[20] China's use of naval power to preserve its vital interests is already being perceived by the other powers as causing a security imbalance in the region. It is thus being factored in a major way in the strategic calculuses of India, the US and others. Submarines, at present, give China a 'short-run relief' with the prospect of acquiring a 'capability' of deploying its naval forces in the Indian Ocean by 2020–2025.

Being the world's second largest economy and having very high dependence on imported oil—all of which passes through the strategic channels located in the Indian Ocean—China perceives the need to have close ties with the Bay's littoral states.[21] China is thus gradually but purposefully expanding its economic and political influence among states in the region and is being inevitably drawn into competing with India and the US. The formidable expansion of Asian infrastructure projects is a new development that gives an increased importance to the Indian Ocean for China. New ports, air routes, roads, rail systems and pipelines now traverse Asia from West to the East, providing a greater access to the landmass of

Eurasia and the Indian Ocean littoral. This generates greater commercial traffic, and strategic cooperation as well as competition. China is keen in engaging commercially to tap these opportunities.

China recognises the dominance of the United States and India in the Indian Ocean. China's strategy is to develop extensive links with the littoral states such as Myanmar, Sri Lanka and Bangladesh. The BCIM initiative is important in this context as regards China's connectivity plan.[22] Since late 2013, China has been promoting its 'Maritime Silk Route' (MSR) initiative as a proposed oceanic complement[23] to its various overland 'Silk Route' projects. The proposal appears to envisage a system of linked ports, infrastructure projects and special economic zones in Southeast Asia and the northern Indian Ocean. If implemented, the initiative would bind countries in the Bay of Bengal and the northern Indian Ocean much closer to the Chinese economy. Although China has long claimed that its interests in the Indian Ocean region are purely economic, it is increasingly clear that the MSR could have a major impact on the strategic balance in the Bay. China has been trying to connect its underdeveloped western provinces to the world economy by gaining access to the Bay. There have been concerns in New Delhi and Washington about the defence cooperation and port infrastructural development between China and the various Bay states leading to a considerable manoeuvring among China, India and the United States.[24]

American Interests

Security relations in and around the Bay region are perceived by the US as having significant implications for its 'Asia pivot strategy'. In the past several years, the US has developed a new interest driven by a mix of geo-strategic, economic and security considerations, in the Bay of Bengal. The US expects that Bangladesh and other states adjoining the Bay in the Indian Ocean should not be under the dominant influence of China. These states should build their own capacity to defend their borders and coasts and develop partnership with the US for the security of what it calls the 'Indo-Pacific corridor'. The US hopes that the Bay 'community' should not relapse into chaotic and unstable conditions and that the countries comprising it should take advantage of the US security assistance programme that aims to "better control their borders and coastline and better deal with natural disasters and transnational security threats".[25] This means that the US seeks to build security relationships and capabilities in the Bay of Bengal in a manner that accords a due consideration to India's imperatives. This includes avoiding or minimising any overt US military presence that could be perceived as impinging upon India's core interests in the Bay. An understanding about respective security objectives and responsibilities in the Bay of Bengal forms part of a more cooperative overall strategic relationship that the US intends to develop with the present government in India.

Perception of the Other Bay States

The strategic competition among the major powers in the Bay offers opportunities as well as challenges to other maritime states such as Bangladesh, Myanmar and Sri Lanka in managing their relationships and courses of action in the Ocean. These littorals states are attempting to leverage their geostrategic location in the Bay by using the aforementioned competition to their advantage.[26] They are trying to give equal priority to their engagements with the major powers. In this context, the perceived India–China or China–US rivalry does not disturb the overall stability; instead, it provides the other littorals a bargaining chip for their increased significance and role in the realisation of the major powers' larger strategic ambitions. To a certain extent, all the littorals have scope to facilitate connectivity, contribute to energy security and provide larger markets for trade to the major regional and extra-regional players. In return, these nations benefit from infrastructural development, financial assistance, integration, naval or military modernisation, etc.

The smaller maritime neighbours are giving close attention especially to India as it consolidates its ambitions in the Indian Ocean. India has actively taken steps to cement partnerships with most of the smaller neighbours in recent years.[27] At the same time, these countries occasionally find difficulty in navigating independent policy paths when they are at odds with India's perspectives.

In recent years, India has been generous in its overtures, contributing to the smaller countries' maritime domain awareness capabilities and dispute resolutions. Prime Minister Modi's government has given high priority to develop close relations with neighbours, especially, Bangladesh, Sri Lanka, Maldives, and Myanmar as well as the island nations further west in the Indian Ocean, i.e. Mauritius and Seychelles.[28] However, maritime cooperation has been limited with Bangladesh and Myanmar as compared to India's interactions with the other Indian Ocean neighbours. Moreover, in reference to Bangladesh, other major powers continue to dominate as defence suppliers—for example, the US provided the Bangladesh Navy with two large ships (former Coast Guard cutters), and China is to sell Bangladesh two Ming-class submarines in addition to building ships and supplying defence hardware. India is, however, building on the momentum of Prime Minister Modi's visit to Bangladesh in June 2015 which saw an MOU signed on Coast Guard cooperation by proposing a bilateral naval exercise, annual navy staff talks, and regular Coast Guard exercises. On balance, however, most of these littoral countries are gradually developing politico-military ties with India, which can be expected to continue to grow as India works to further build its capabilities in the Indian Ocean. India's crisis response operations are well appreciated by neighbours, while India's capacity-building efforts are being directed towards improving these countries' maritime forces and for advancing regional security and cooperation.

Future Outlook

The maritime domain offers the potential for providing important 'building blocks' for regional cooperation and dialogue that would contribute to security in the Bay region. In this regard, the littoral states need to make an unambiguous declaration that the freedom of navigation and unimpeded commerce shall be ensured to all stakeholders in the global commons. The medium-term maritime trajectory in the Bay region seems cooperative as we examine the triangular dynamics among the United States, China and India. The perception of the 'China threat' mainly derives from a fear of China's distinct political system and its astonishing rise—both in scale and speed. But when analysed in relation to intention, capability or aspiration, it is clear that the potential threat of China has always been over-exaggerated. Moreover, the US and India have convergent Indian Ocean strategies or 'they are in entente' in ensuring stability in the Bay and the Indo-Pacific corridor.

Confidence building is the key at this juncture for unlocking the potential of cooperation among the Bay states or the community. It is clear that India has acquired substantial maritime capability, but it is yet to generate enough confidence in the capitals of the surrounding nations of the Bay of Bengal. It is therefore, imperative that cooperative regime building attempts should start on the relatively modest level of confidence-building measures. This new approach should emphasise the facilitation of cooperation in functional areas which will in turn help the littoral states to build trust and move beyond the South Asian stereotype of non-engagement by cultivating a habit of dialogue and cooperation at various levels. These areas include disaster relief, search and rescue (SAR), sustainable development of marine resources, fisheries protection and the fight against terrorism and piracy. All these measures can be subsumed under the label 'maritime governance'.

In fact, a regional governance framework is very much needed at this point that will lead to good order in the Bay, concerted action for use and protection of global commons and an increased maritime domain awareness. Institutionalisation of cooperation is very much needed now. A number of regional institutions such as the IORA, IONS, Milan, Galle

Dialogue that exist for the Indian Ocean need to be invigorated to promote bilateral and multilateral cooperation. In fact, greater cooperation can only help change perceptions and mindsets in ways that substantially reduce the chance of conflict. Exchange of information, capacity building and the provision of technical assistance amongst the IORA member-states is an important element for cooperation in enhancing the political will to address the challenges of maritime safety and security. The establishment of a regular forum for dialogue between stakeholders on security and safety should therefore be further explored. IORA may also look into the greater involvement of external stakeholders and other regional and sub-regional groupings. It could also consider collaborating with relevant UN agencies such as UNEP, IOC-UNESCO, etc.

Regional civil maritime organisations also offer a more effective and less-politicised vehicle for engagement. Cooperation between public and private stakeholders could promote harmonisation and implementation of maritime safety and security regulations and foster innovation and initiatives towards creating a common information-sharing environment for maritime security. Major energy producers and consumers in cooperation with navies of the littoral states can also work to increase 'maritime domain awareness' by integrating information on key energy assets and the locations of severe natural phenomena, piracy and terrorist threats along major sea lanes and production areas. In this context, the experience of the Regional Cooperation Agreement on Combating Piracy and Armed Robbery against Ships in Asia (ReCAAP) that consists of three pillars—information sharing, capacity building and cooperative arrangements—could be very useful.

A cooperative regional mechanism for good order in the Bay is needed which will shape a new architecture of regional maritime governance through which littoral states are able to pursue their maritime interests and develop energy, infrastructure and resources in a peaceful manner and in accordance with international law and practice. The Maritime Doctrine of Bangladesh stresses the need for regional cooperation in this regard and maintains that stability in the entire Indian Ocean will hinge largely on how India manages its maritime rise. Clearly, India seems to realise that a 'zero-sum' mindset is irrelevant today. A robust, but not exclusive, Indian maritime presence would surely facilitate the convergence of interests with littoral states as well as China and the United States. The strategic engagements of India or the United States, therefore, must aim to enhance cooperation for stability, peace and development reinforced by strategic trust and reflected in concrete and constructive policies and actions. Political will and vision must pave the way for a new order in the Ocean which is so vital for the peace and prosperity of the region.

Prime Minister Modi in his March 2015 visit to Seychelles and Mauritius seemed to show such vision when he declared, "Our goal is to seek a climate of trust and transparency; respect for international maritime rules and norms by all countries; sensitivity to each other's interests; peaceful resolution of maritime issues; and increase in maritime cooperation."

Notes

1. Brewster, David. "The Bay of Bengal: The Indo-Pacific's New Zone of Competition", *The Strategist*, Australian Strategic Policy Institute, 2 Dec 2014, http://www.aspistrategist.org.au/the-bay-of-bengal-the-indo-pacifics-new-zone-of-competition/, and ; Samarnayake, Nilanthi. *The Long Littoral Project: Bay of Bengal:A Maritime Perspective on Indo-Pacific Security*. Washington, Center for Naval Analyses, September 2012, https://www.cna.org/CNA_files/PDF/IRP-2012-U-002319-Final.pdf.
2. Khurana, Gurpreet S. "Common Public Good at Sea: Evolving Architecture in the Indo-Pacific Region", IFR Issue Brief, National Maritime Foundation, New Delhi, 04 January 2016, http://www.maritimeindia.org/View%20Profile/635875578606062366.pdf.
3. Amrith, Sunil S. *Crossing the Bay of Bengal: The Furies of Nature and the Fortunes of Migrants*, Cambridge, Massachusetts: Harvard University Press, 2013.
4. Brewster, David. "The Bay of Bengal: A New Locus for Strategic Competition in Asia," Asia Pacific Bulletin, 15 May 2014, *East-West Center*, http://www.eastwestcenter.org/sites/default/files/private/apb263_0.pdf ; also, Bateman, S. Book Review of "Asian Maritime Power in the 21st Century-Strategic Transactions: China, India and Southeast Asia", *Journal of Indian Ocean Region*, 2012, 8 (1), 99-101;
5. *Encyclopaedia Britannica*, Bay of Bengal.
6. Blakeley, Ian. "Exploration Asia: Bay of Bengal", *Geo ExPro*, Vol. 7, No. 6, 2010, http://www.geoexpro.com/articles/2010/06/bay-of-bengal
7. First IORA Ministerial Blue Economy Conference was held in Mauritius from 2–3 September 2015.
8. Amrith, Sunil. "The Bay of Bengal, in Peril from Climate Change", *New York Times*, 13 October 2013, http://www.nytimes.com/2013/10/14/opinion/the-bay-of-bengal-in-peril-from-climate-change.html?ref=international&_r=2&
9. "The Bay of Bengal : New Bay Dawning", *The Economist*, 27 April 2013, http://www.economist.com/news/asia/21576721-harbours-eastern-lobe-indian-ocean-could-transform-economic-geography-asia-new
10. Ibid.
11. S.D. Muni. "India and the Security of Asia", Institute of South Asian Studies, National University of Singapore, 2012, http://www.isis.org.my/files/2012/26APR/PS3_S_D_MUNI.pdf
12. Amrith. "The Bay of Bengal", Note 8.
13. Mishra, Raghavendra. "Maritime Military Context of the US Rebalance: Strategic Basis and Prognosis", *Maritime Affairs*, Journal of the National Maritime Foundation of India, Volume 10, Issue 2, 2014, 52-76.
14. Rahman, Ataur. "Resource Potential, Security Scenario and China's Strategic Initiatives in the Bay of Bengal", China Study Group (CSG- Research Paper), 2013.

15. Tweed, David and N.C Bipindra. "Submarine Killers: India's $61 Billion Warning to China", *BloombergBusiness*, 29 July 2015, http://www.bloomberg.com/news/articles/2015-07-28/submarine-killers-showcase-india-s-61-billion-warning-to-china. This report stated that India plans to add at least 100 new warships, including two aircraft carriers, as well as three nuclear powered submarines capable of firing nuclear-tipped ballistic missiles.
16. "Mr. Modi's Ocean View", *The Hindu*, 17 March 2015, http://www.thehindu.com/opinion/editorial/mr-modis-ocean-view/article7000182.ece.
17. "Ensuring Secure Seas: Indian Maritime Security Strategy", Integrated Headquarters, Ministry of Defence (Navy), 2015, New Delhi.
18. Ramachandran, Sudha. "Indian Navy Pumps up Eastern Muscle", *Asia Times*, 20 August 2011, http://www.atimes.com/atimes/South_Asia/MH20Df02.html. This article brought out that the enhanced attention being paid to the Eastern Command has been prompted in part by China's looming naval presence in the Bay of Bengal. It is part of India's two decades-long effort to play a significant role in the security architecture of the Indo-Pacific. The Eastern Command is in charge of India's nuclear submarines including the *INS Arihant* based at Visakhapatnam.
19. Brewster, "The Bay of Bengal", Note 1.
20. Sakhuja, Vijay. "Blue Economy: China Explores Bay of Bengal Partnership", *South Asia Defence and Strategic Review*, 29 July 2015, http://www.defstrat.com/exec/frmArticleDetails.aspx?DID=555
21. Holslag, J. "The Reluctant Pretender: China's Evolving Presence in the Indian Ocean", *Journal of Indian Ocean Region*, Vol. 9, No. 1, 04, 2013, 42-52.
22. Brewster, David. "The Bay of Bengal: The Maritime Silk Route and China's Naval Ambitions", *The Strategist*, Australian Strategic Policy Institute, 9 December 2014, http://www.aspistrategist.org.au/the-bay-of-bengal-the-maritime-silk-route-and-chinas-naval-ambitions/.
23. Mohan, Raja C. "Losing the Bay of Bengal", *Indian Express*, 4 March 2014, http://indianexpress.com/article/opinion/columns/losing-the-bay-of-bengal/.
24. Karim, Mohd. Aminul. "China's Proposed Maritime Silk Road: Challenges and Opportunities with Special Reference to the Bay of Bengal Region", *Pacific Focus*, Vol. 30, No. 3 (December 2015), 297–319.
25. Khurana, Gurpreet S., "Why is India so Coy about China's Maritime Silk-Road?" *The Wire*, 9 June 2015, http://thewire.in/2015/06/09/why-is-india-so-coy-about-chinas-maritime-silk-road-3522/.
26. Andrew J. Shapiro, US Assistant Secretary of State who led the delegation to Bangladesh in the first-ever Security Dialogue between the two countries in Dhaka on 19 April 2012.
27. Brewster. "The Bay of Bengal", Note 1.
28. Vijay Sakhuja. "Indian Ocean: Modi on a Maritime Pilgrimage", INDIA – ARTICLES #4844, 2 March 2015, Institute of Peace and Conflict Studies, http://www.ipcs.org/article/india/indian-ocean-modi-on-a-maritime-pilgrimage-4844.html.

12. A Tour de Horizon

Satish Soni

As the Commander-in-Chief of the host Command, I wish to thank our overseas friends and the foreign navies for joining us at the Navy's Eastern Naval Command. More than anything else, I hope that that the International Fleet Review has been a memorable experience.

This Conference has been one of the highlights of the International Fleet Review and all would agree that the last couple of days have been most educative and informative. Interactions between delegates, other participants and the audience at formal and informal levels have provided an opportunity to all for presenting their perspectives on maritime issues, thereby clearing the fog to some extent.

For some, this Conference maybe the first visit to India's eastern coast; a coast that has its own unique history and flavour. Buddhism and Hinduism spread to the Far East from these very shores. The ancient Buddhist sites at Bhavikonda and Thotlakonda here in this city are one such example. A Hindu shrine in China dating back to the eleventh century, the Angkor Wat temple complex in Cambodia, the Hindu mythological bird Garuda as the Indonesian emblem—hark back to the ancient mariners who interacted beyond India's eastern shores across the Bay of Bengal through the Straits of Malacca into the South China Sea, and beyond. It would thus be obvious that India's eastern seaboard has its own dynamics which are in many ways similar but unique, given the nature of interactions across a geographically disparate region with diverse forms of governance and socio-cultural, economic and ideational practices.

The organisers—especially the National Maritime Foundation—need to be complimented for selecting such an appropriate theme for this Conference; one that effectively captures the spirit, flavour and essence of the International Fleet Review. If there was one common thread running through the discussions over the last two days, it was that security, growth and prosperity of maritime nations has but one driver—that of cooperation and partnerships at sea.

The opening remarks by the Chairman, National Maritime Foundation, Admiral DK Joshi, set the tone for the Conference. He raised some excellent critical questions; some were addressed by the speakers, whilst others gave us much food for thought. As he also mentioned, there are no easy answers. However, getting all stakeholders together on a common platform, as attempted here, helps immensely and sets the agenda for further deliberations.

The speakers also need to be complimented for putting across their thoughts in a logical and lucid manner. The papers presented were of an extremely high quality, and the discussions that followed were intelligent and thought-provoking. It is clear that all consider maritime cooperation to be of immense importance and the way ahead—or as Admiral Anup Singh put it, the '*Hi Way*'. The Fleet Review itself is a most apt example. That so many nations have come together is testimony to the fact that the so-called 'soft' roles of the navies—Diplomatic and Benign—are fast gaining pre-eminence over the traditional 'hard' roles. Rear Admiral Raja Menon also expressed the opinion that the war-fighting role of navies is on the decline; Rear Admiral Goldrick hit the nail on its head when he stated that navies by their nature and the medium in which they operate, possess a historical and cultural affinity for operations other than war to a far greater degree than is true for the other armed forces.

There also appears to be a consensus that there are far too many issues—some fairly complex—in the maritime domain. There is also a sense that whilst cooperative mechanisms may look good on the drawing board, they may be not as easy to implement—more so in the Indo-Pacific. Professor Ataur Rahman used an interesting term: 'the South Asian stereotype of non-engagement'. Institution of a regional maritime forum for the Bay of Bengal, as the Professor also recommends, is probably a good first step in this direction.

The Asia-Pacific appears to be experiencing a wave of maritime nationalism. There are several indicators: infrastructure development on disputed maritime features, unilateral declaration of Air Defence Identification Zones, nationalisation of disputed islands, a distinct hardening of stance in Policy Papers and strategy documents, frequent deployment of naval forces at extended ranges, strident reactions to transgressions into one's claimed waters—perceived or otherwise—reinterpretation of the constitution, reworking of defence alliances, increased defence spending, enhancement of naval capabilities including procurement of submarines and expeditionary platforms and so on. Some of you even predict an arms race in the making, and Admiral Beaussant forecasts that half of the world's submarines in 2030 will belong to the Asian navies. Obviously, nations are striving hard to provide maritime security to their people.

There has also been a marked increase in levels of maritime cooperation by way of bilateral and multilateral summits, exchange of hardware and defence technology, joint naval exercises, staff talks, port visits and visits by Service officers. For example, the Rim of the Pacific (RIMPAC) Exercise off Hawaii in 2014 saw participation by more than 45 countries; the Malabar exercise has progressively increased in terms of its scope and complexity and there have been several 'firsts' in terms of bilateral naval exercises—the ones between India and Australia, and India and Indonesia, being recent examples.

However, it is also useful to emphasise the contradictions. Despite the fact that nations today are investing more time, effort and resources towards maritime security, and are also cooperating more than ever before, many think tanks—and indeed some of the speakers here—predict rising tensions and increasing levels of insecurity. Professor Geoffrey Till mentioned that the Indo-Pacific region has a large number of differing national maritime objectives which cannot be easily reconciled. Admiral Octavian added that 42 per cent of the global conflict can be associated with countries in the Indian Ocean Region and that a third of the territorial disputes in Asia are over offshore features, with only one-third of them having been settled. These statements are revealing. Obviously, there is a disconnect suggesting that the approach by countries in providing maritime security is less than perfect.

As the Conference concludes, it is considered useful to reiterate some of the salient issues. No one country can take ownership or responsibility for ensuring maritime security, no matter how big or small an area; this point was made quite forcefully by Professor Renfrew Christie. This is particularly applicable in the South China Sea (SCS) and the Indian Ocean Region where the issues are more about maritime security than anything else. Maritime security has to be a collaborative effort.

Whilst the overall dependence on the sea trade and size of the merchant marine are increasing, the numbers of warships available for providing security are on the decline. Rear Admiral Antoine Beaussant and Professor Christie also mentioned the fact that traditional powers which have always guaranteed protection at sea may not continue to do so at the same level due to a variety of reasons. This suggests the need for a capacity build-up, as also collaborative efforts between navies and other maritime enforcement agencies.

Next, the resolution of differences requires an adherence to the universally accepted conventions and laws and a mature and sensible 'rules-based' approach by all stakeholders. Admiral Octavian spoke about arbitration as an effective dispute-settlement mechanism. He has also suggested utilising the San Remo Manual as a legal basis for this mechanism—a most useful suggestion that merits consideration.

A recent example where arbitration worked quite well is the resolution of the longstanding Indo-Bangladesh Maritime Boundary dispute in the northern Bay of Bengal. The verdict may not have been to the complete satisfaction of India or for that matter Bangladesh; however, it was accepted in 'good spirit' by both parties. The longstanding maritime dispute between Bangladesh and Myanmar has also been resolved and consequently, as Professor Rahman so aptly puts it, the maritime atmosphere in the Bay of Bengal has indeed changed for the better. Yet another case where arbitration has resulted in a historic breakthrough is in the case of the 'Agreed Cornerstones' agreement between Germany and the Netherlands. This, along with the Bay of Bengal arbitrations, is a most encouraging example of resolving long outstanding and seemingly intractable disputes through a non-traditional 'commonsensical' approach and political compromise.

A few speakers have highlighted the inadequacy of existing conventions and mechanisms. Professor Katahara was of the opinion that the efficacy and scope of certain 'rules of the game' remain limited and that a stronger rule-based international order is the need of the day. Vice Admiral Anup Singh questioned the effectiveness of the 1984 United Convention on the Law of the Sea (UNCLOS) where he argued that the Convention has not been effective in the emergence of new disputes over the last couple of decades. The Hon'ble Raksha Mantri and Rear Admiral Raja Menon also suggested the need to update and strengthen international treaties and frameworks. These suggestions need serious examination and there is a need to review, and indeed renew, some of the existing international frameworks. It goes without saying that there should be consensus and collaboration to arrive at international norms that are enduring, workable and—just as importantly— universally acceptable.

Nations need to exercise due care in developing infrastructure with military connotations within their boundaries and overseas since such actions can easily be misunderstood. They also need to be transparent in their actions, especially when it comes to deployment of military units for peacetime missions. As Professor Till emphasised, the lack of transparency can bring about unintended consequences as is being seen in case of China's 'One Belt One Road' proposal. The possibility of a hidden 'operational consequence' is preventing nations from fully endorsing this initiative even though it may have benign and trade-related implications. In his paper, Professor Hailin's says, "China considers the intensification of the South China Sea issue as an obstacle and threat that would affect the implementation of China's foreign strategies, especially the 'Belt and Road'". Evidently, a perception persists about 'inadequate clarity' that needs to be addressed.

Speakers including Admiral Anup Singh and Admiral Goldrick stressed that bigger nations must assess and accept the aspirations of smaller countries and assist in capability enhancement to enable them to contribute towards maritime security. Smaller nations, especially developing ones, may not have the luxury of diverting scarce resources towards defence and security. They must not be pressurised by circumstances or otherwise to spare capital on capacity building and should be assisted by their 'more enabled' neighbours. In this context, Prof. Rahman needs special mention for his generous comments about India's overtures in its immediate maritime neighbourhood. India has provided ships and aircraft to our maritime neighbours that are not as well equipped. India also deploys ships for patrolling the Exclusive Economic Zones of nations that lack the wherewithal to manage their huge maritime entitlements on their own. India pays for its logistics, does not seek basing rights and perceives such efforts as pure benign cooperative initiatives. Further, India's training establishments have an annual turnover of over 800 foreign trainees, with expenses being borne by the host nation.

Almost all speakers have recommended the need for dialogue and more interaction. The Indian Navy took the initiative towards one such mechanism in the form of the Indian Ocean Naval Symposium or IONS, which has done well in the relatively fewer years of its existence, with a fairly good recall value. While India was the initiator, the institutional leadership subsequently passed on to the UAE, South Africa, Australia and, presently, Bangladesh. There is need for strengthening this mechanism by taking it to the next level wherein it can play a more active policy and functional role.

Singapore's International Data Fusion Centre is another example where a Navy-led mechanism has been quite successful, although on a smaller scale. Recently, it played an important role during search operations for the MH 370 aircraft wherein it was able to sanitise large ocean areas by tapping into its linkages with the merchant marine. Another example is that of the Malacca security mechanisms. As the Chief of the Naval Staff also suggested, a similar template could be adopted at a higher, more operational level, possibly starting with a formally established mechanism for coordinating Humanitarian Aid and Disaster Relief (HADR) operations in this region. There is also a need for setting up a mechanism for intelligence sharing, especially for dealing with the threat posed by non-state actors.

The topic of Maritime Domain Awareness and the potential it has for facilitating cooperation amongst maritime nations has been discussed at length. Developments over the last few years have been encouraging and it seems that a scenario involving an exchange of White Shipping information between regional navies could be institutionalised.

Finally, it is felt that the navies need to be able to 'talk' to each other better, especially at the tactical level. This aspect also found mention in the talks by some speakers including Gen. Dan Leaf who shared some good insights on the subject. Multinational deployments at a short notice for a common mission must not grope in the dark when they meet each other at sea. This leads to a question pertaining to common Manoeuvring Instructions, Signal Codes and even communications equipment in future. It may seem somewhat ambitious right now; although, certainly not impossible. Exchanges between navies have been stepped up in recent times; however, regional navies still have some distance to cover in terms of seamless interoperability. Conferences such as this help flag collective challenges and hopefully play a part in reducing the inertia sometimes seen in getting the cooperative initiatives on road.

I am in complete agreement with General Leaf that English needs to be pursued as the medium of language of communication between navies. The Indian Navy lays a lot of emphasis on language training and all its officers and sailors are able to communicate in English within a matter of few years of their recruitment. This helps us immensely during joint exercises.

The fact that the International Fleet Review has witnessed participation by over 50 countries is an acknowledgement of the tremendous potential that the Navy-led initiatives have for getting maritime nations on to a common platform. This is also a most appropriate example of, and to quote Professor Till, the 'natural fraternity amongst sailors'. His generous comments about the conduct of the Fleet Review here at Visakhapatnam are noteworthy in this regard. All would agree that IFR 16 has definitely played its part in terms of a constructive maritime engagement.

[Editor's Note: Adapted from the valedictory address delivered at the International maritime Conference on 08 February 2016]

Index